# Tech for All

# LIBRARY INFORMATION TECHNOLOGY ASSOCIATION (LITA) GUIDES

Marta Mestrovic Deyrup, PhD
Acquisitions Editor, Library Information and Technology Association, a division of the American Library Association

The Library Information Technology Association (LITA) Guides provide information and guidance on topics related to cutting edge technology for library and IT specialists.

Written by top professionals in the field of technology, the guides are sought after by librarians wishing to learn a new skill or to become current in today's best practices.

Each book in the series has been overseen editorially since conception by LITA and reviewed by LITA members with special expertise in the specialty area of the book.

Established in 1966, LITA is the division of the American Library Association (ALA) that provides its members and the library and information science community as a whole with a forum for discussion, an environment for learning, and a program for actions on the design, development, and implementation of automated and technological systems in the library and information science field.

Approximately 25 LITA Guides were published by Neal-Schuman and ALA between 2007 and 2015. Rowman & Littlefield took over publication of the series beginning in late 2015. Books in the series published by Rowman & Littlefield are:

*Digitizing Flat Media: Principles and Practices*
*The Librarian's Introduction to Programming Languages*
*Library Service Design: A LITA Guide to Holistic Assessment, Insight, and Improvement*
*Data Visualization: A Guide to Visual Storytelling for Librarians*
*Mobile Technologies in Libraries: A LITA Guide*
*Innovative LibGuides Applications*
*Integrating LibGuides into Library Websites*
*Protecting Patron Privacy: A LITA Guide*
*The LITA Leadership Guide: The Librarian as Entrepreneur, Leader, and Technologist*
*Using Social Media to Build Library Communities: A LITA Guide*
*Managing Library Technology: A LITA Guide*
*The LITA Guide to No- or Low-Cost Technology Tools for Libraries*
*Big Data Shocks: An Introduction to Big Data for Librarians and Information Professionals*
*The Savvy Academic Librarian's Guide to Technological Innovation: Moving Beyond the Wow Factor*
*The LITA Guide to Augmented Reality in Libraries*
*Digital Curation Projects Made Easy: A Step-By-Step Guide for Libraries, Archives, and Museums*
*Library Technology Planning for Today and Tomorrow: A LITA Guide*
*Tech for All: Moving beyond the Digital Divide*

# Tech for All

## Moving beyond the Digital Divide

Edited by Lauren Comito

ROWMAN & LITTLEFIELD
*Lanham • Boulder • New York • London*

Published by Rowman & Littlefield
An imprint of The Rowman & Littlefield Publishing Group, Inc.
4501 Forbes Boulevard, Suite 200, Lanham, Maryland 20706
www.rowman.com

6 Tinworth Street, London SE11 5AL, United Kingdom

British Library Cataloguing in Publication Information Available

**Library of Congress Cataloging-in-Publication Data**

Names: Comito, Lauren, editor.
Title: Tech for all : moving beyond the digital divide / edited by Lauren
    Comito.
Description: Lanham : Rowman & Littlefield, [2018] | Series: LITA guides |
    Includes bibliographical references and index.
Identifiers: LCCN 2018040684 (print) | LCCN 2018053082 (ebook) | ISBN
    9781538122198 (electronic) | ISBN 9781538122174 (cloth : alk. paper) |
    ISBN 9781538122181 (pbk. : alk. paper)
Subjects: LCSH: Public access computers in libraries. | Internet access for
    library users. | Makerspaces in libraries. | Digital divide. | Computer
    literacy. | Internet literacy.
Classification: LCC Z678.93.P83 (ebook) | LCC Z678.93.P83 T43 2018 (print) |
    DDC 025.50285--dc23
LC record available at https://lccn.loc.gov/2018040684

Printed in the United States of America

# Contents

# List of Figures

# List of Tables

# Foreword

*Matthew Kopel*

Let's start with the obvious: Leveling the playing field is a tremendously difficult task. It isn't just about having the access to the resources we need, or those we'll need tomorrow, but about ensuring that patrons have the language and context to be able to know what they need, and the librarians and community advocates to respond to and facilitate those requests and opportunities. All communities deserve a fair shake, meaning that there should be no limits on what patrons can ask for. We've seen more and more changes in our libraries and community spaces as the world has changed around us, more resources online, more options for access to the resources we provide.

In some cases, there are champions who will push for progress and set the pace for change. *Tech for All* is a showcase not only of great ideas, but of folks who are working together to make those ideas responsive to requests, scalable to fit the communities being served, and representative of attainable ideals. We don't need "The IT Crowd" to show up, but to provide better training and professional development. Not all libraries will define the makerspace of their dreams in the same way, which means our makers and fabricators must take a broad approach to what those services might look like. Building web savvy library staff won't mean that everyone is a developer, but instead have a foundational knowledge complemented with robust, reliable broadband connections in order to help students, small businesses, and all other patrons be able to build and explore without restriction.

The folks who've contributed chapters to this volume are intelligent, courageous, and inspiring professionals. I've had the privilege to work with several of them, and cannot express how excited I am for you to be inspired by them. They will share the "ah ha!" of using Linux instead of Windows when the use case permits, allowing for larger computer labs, refurbishing workshops and lending programs to meet expanded community need on a budget. They will make the parallels more clear between patron training programs and the professional development needs staff face across our institutions and spaces. These folks are working in different environs, with different funding levels, different local needs, and different amounts of buy-in (both internally and externally). They're folks who came into this arena of work with a plan, and folks who've needed to make up the plan as they went along. They're people who care enough not just to do the work, but to bring it to the table for discussion and criticism, which is a tremendous challenge in itself.

And then we have you, the person who picked up this book. Maybe it was at a booth at a conference, or perhaps you're burning some time while monitoring the computer lab. Perhaps you're reading this for your MSLIS, or you're a seasoned veteran of the library looking for resources to fit the chorus of calls from your patrons for new programs and opportunities. Perhaps you think this is important. I really hope that you do, because in the chapters of this book you'll find not just concrete examples of folks doing the work and helping their whole libraries learn, but you'll see the fomentation of the sea change many of us came to the profession to help along.

We stand on the shoulders of giants and luminaries, some who've been around and others who have come in as disruptive forces for change, answering the call and setting the bar. The editor of this volume was a major inspiration to me when she hacked together whereinqueens.org. When I see Jessamyn West's TILT email pop into my inbox, I drop everything, go into lockdown, and begin to prepare myself to learn. When I sat with Carrie Coogan of Kansas City Public Library and Elizabeth Lindsay of Byte Back on a panel, I did my best to shut up and appreciate that I had the best seat in the house to hear about how the pros get the work done. When Nicole Umayum at the Arizona State Library tells me about progress in their hotspot program, or when Sandy Tharp-Thee sends me pictures of the new computer labs she's set up for tribes in Oklahoma, I am reminded of what we're all really here for.

Our work is just getting started. We need to add your voice to the growing choir, we need your best practices and innovative responses and problem solving added to those contained within. We need more projects like Internet2's Broadband Assessment Toolkit forthcoming toolkit for rural and tribal libraries, and we need more attention paid to the issue at our conferences. We need professional development organizations to prioritize exposure to new and disruptive services, and development of technological competencies. We need your strength and determination to make sure that each of our spaces and communities has what it needs to bring every patron and partner to the table. Read up and share actively. Make #techforall trend at every conference and reconstruct your definition of digital inclusion and equity at every opportunity.

Finally, that these folks are grouped together reminds us of the most important thing: We're not working in a vacuum. You don't have to reinvent the wheel, but instead we all have to do a better job of sharing what we know, what we've learned, how we responded, and how we made it through one leg or another of the journey of library transformation. We're all in this together, for our libraries, for our patrons, for our communities, and for each other. Don't forget to share, and to shine a light on your peers you catch doing something right. No matter what trends bubble up to the surface, what technologies evolve and become crucial, we know one thing for certain: We all have a lot of learning yet to do.

# Preface

*Lauren Comito*

The role of the library as technology facilitator has been well established by the efforts of library professionals over the last few decades. The world has been changing, and access to basic services that members of our communities need to live their lives has been moved increasingly online. Public libraries have been working to respond to the needs of their service areas and communities by providing access to the technological tools that can make a difference. And yet, like the rest of society, libraries have vastly differing resource levels, leading to some libraries providing more access to emerging technologies than others. We know that members of our communities with easy access to technology and the knowledge to use it well are able to participate in society more easily that those without. These inequities don't just hold back individuals, they hold us all back.

Fixing this means making efforts to extend services providing access to emerging technologies into economically disadvantaged and traditionally underserved areas and addressing the needs of special populations. That will look different in every community. There is no one solution to providing equitable access to technology resources, especially in local, taxpayer-funded institutions. In reality, sometimes the solution is money, sometimes it is time, and sometimes it is a great idea, combined with just the right person with the drive to make it happen.

The solutions presented in this book all have one thing in common, a directed response to community needs. The authors in this book give real-world examples of libraries going the extra mile to bring more than just email access to their communities, regardless of economic status or geographic distribution. Many of the programs detailed in this book are funded by grants, so the first chapter will describe grant writing in the context of technology projects.

Then in part II, we will cover issues related to physical access to technology through case studies of libraries that brought new equipment to underserved or geographically remote areas and a way to use Linux to expand access to PCs in a small library, that could be replicated elsewhere.

In part III, we will look at training solutions for both patrons and staff. Training can provide a bridge over the digital divide for library patrons. This section will cover ways in which technology training can be offered to make library services more robust. Moving into part IV, we will look at the holy grail of emerging technologies in libraries, the Makerspace. As libraries start to develop Makerspaces and creation labs, they tend to crop up in wealthier and more resource rich areas. This section will show ways libraries have built maker programs in communities with fewer resources. And finally, in part V, we will look at ways that libraries can provide expanded workforce and business assistance using technology.

After reading this book, public librarians should have a set of practical ideas to address the issue of access to emerging technologies in their own communities. One thing every chapter in this book has in common is an idea, a funding source, and a person or team of people with the passion to do the work. My hope is that you as the reader will take away the confidence to try something new yourself.

# Acknowledgments

This book would not have been possible without the assistance and forbearance of many people. I'd first like to thank my husband, John, and daughter, Tara, for allowing me to disappear for hours at a time without complaint. You are both incredibly patient. Thank you to Matthew Kopel for helping me reach so many amazing contributors, and Christian Zabriskie for, as always, helping me turn my writing into something readable.

And finally, I'd like to acknowledge all the patrons whose drive and passions inspire me and make going to work every day a joy.

# Introduction

## Digital Equity in Libraries

*Lauren Comito*

Over the last twenty years, technology and computers have seeped their way into everyday life. A basic knowledge of how to use technology has become necessary for daily activities, but opportunities for access to that technology and the opportunity to learn how to integrate it into our lives have often been lacking. Since the advent of the personal computer, libraries have provided access and training in digital literacy. Nearly every public library in the United States provides computers for public use, and across the nation, people use computers and internet access in libraries every day. Many libraries provide classes in basic computer use, word processing, email, and in some cases, more advanced subjects like social media, graphic design, or coding. Libraries have become a place where the community expects to find computers, printers, and technology assistance, and it has quickly become a main part of our missions. According to the Pew Research Center's Libraries 2016 study, "Public libraries, many Americans say, should offer programs to teach people digital skills (80 percent think libraries should definitely do this) and help patrons learn how to use new creative technologies like 3-D printers (50 percent)" (Horrigan, 2017).

It's not surprising that so many people see libraries as a place for these activities. If there is one thing libraries and librarians are good at it is breaking down barriers, both within our communities and for the people in them. When personal computers and internet access became necessary for everyday life, we figured out how to provide them. As the last mile of broadband stretches out into rural areas, we look at ways to become hubs for our communities. We hunt down grants and shake money out of our budgets to provide more and more services to our communities, discovering the needs they have and filling them the best we can. The impact libraries have made in this area has been amazing, but we can do more. To do this we need to acknowledge the disparities in opportunity and take steps to fix them. This book will give examples of how libraries across the United States are overcoming challenges in their service areas and providing advanced digital literacy training to their communities.

In 2011, four years into my professional career, I joined the team implementing the Broadband Technology Opportunity Program (BTOP) grant at Queens Library as an outreach librarian. As part of the NYC Connected Communities program, we were tasked with expanding access to public computers, creating and implementing computer and job readiness classes, and providing individual assistance to patrons and job seekers in Long Island City, Jamaica, and the Rockaway Peninsula. For those unfamiliar with New York City, these are economically depressed areas that took the brunt of the economic downturn in 2008. We embraced the challenge. The BTOP team set up computer classes in each of our locations, helped patrons through online coursework with Metrix Learning, and provided one-on-one help that patrons needed to stand out in a truly horrible job market. Even with all of that, we were still limited by the amount of funding and staff available. We addressed basic digital literacy very effectively, but we weren't able to do much of the extras.

A few years later I was given a tour of a suburban library with an amazing Makerspace. They had a green screen room, CNC routers, sewing machines, woodworking tools, and at least six 3D printers. It was an amazing space, and I found it incredibly inspiring. By the end of the tour however, I realized that I had been grinding my teeth so much that my jaw ached. It wasn't that the space didn't fit the function of a library, it did; and it wasn't the people, they were lovely. It was the creeping realization that the patrons I work with every day didn't have access to these types of resources and wouldn't in the near future. Why does a library in a predominantly white suburban community have these resources while southern Queens doesn't?

We were still helping with basic daily needs like resumes and unemployment applications. Those services are necessary, and they fill basic human needs, but just because those needs were so pressing, doesn't mean that we shouldn't also be providing an opportunity to dream and create. Libraries are places of creation. They are spaces where the people in a community can come together to build things that are bigger than themselves. Like so many other things in our society, some communities get better tools than others.

In recent years libraries have begun to address digital inclusion, attempting to provide access, services, and training to ensure that everyone in our community is able to participate fully in digital life. The Information Policy & Access Center defines digital inclusion as an "overarching approach to ensure that all members of a community are 'digitally ready'—able to access, use, and understand digital technologies and content without cost, social, accessibility, or other barriers" (Bertot et. al, 2015). Libraries are institutions that aim to level the playing field between our patrons who have money and resources and those who don't. Yes, the majority of libraries offer basic computer classes, like introductions to the PC, internet, and email. Many are even able to offer one-on-one assistance with technology and related activities. Some offer slightly more advanced classes, like Microsoft Office, and how to use various social media platforms. Even libraries are subject to inequality and have to make choices about what types of services to offer. Where one library may be able to invest in a makerspace, another may be struggling just to offer basic computer classes. For example, the average amount of public library funding per capita in New York State as a whole in fiscal year 2013 was $63 (https://www.humanitiesindicators.org/content/indicatorDoc .aspx?i=419), while the average per capita funding between the three library systems in New York City in 2011 was $35 (Giles, 2013: 46). There have been funding increases in New York City since 2011, but not enough to bridge that gap. Funding disparities like these happen for many reasons, but the result is that libraries with less money have to make difficult budget decisions. Fortunately for New York City, large library systems like New York Public Library, Brooklyn Public Library, and Queens Library have the staff and the fundraising structure to apply for and manage large grants that can help make up some of the difference. For small libraries with fewer resources, this is more of a challenge and requires creative solutions.

The organization Makerbridge has developed an excellent map that shows library makerspaces around the world (http://makerbridge.si.umich.edu /makerspaces-in-libraries-museums-map/). Most of the spaces recorded for public libraries, particularly those in urban areas, seem to be in central libraries, not out in smaller neighborhood branches. Makerspaces take up space and cost money. For a library to get the most out of its investment, placing the space in its flagship building is a no-brainer. It does limit the geographic range of participants, however, and requires travel for patrons from outlying neighborhoods to reach the equipment. In contrast, the Carnegie Free Library of Pittsburgh has spread theirs out into three branches and provides pop-up labs in other branches. It's important that we look at transportation as a barrier and try to mitigate that and look for ways to put these resources close enough to our patrons that they can use them. In addition to the centralized location of makerspaces themselves, according to *Library Journal*'s *Maker Programs in Public Libraries* study, "Libraries serving populations under 25,000 are significantly less likely to offer maker services (only 77 percent). Correspondingly, rural and small town libraries are the least likely to offer maker programs" (Maker Programs in Public Libraries, 2017: 4). There may be no way to mitigate the funding disparities between libraries in different areas, but we can make creative choices so that smaller libraries can offer similar programming to that at a more well-off library.

Why is this important? If everyone has a smartphone containing the whole world in their pocket, why should libraries keep pushing to provide more digital literacy services? Why provide new or advanced services? The simple fact is that not everyone does have that world in their pocket. Even when they do have them, smartphones don't allow their users to do things like learn to code or fill out job applications, at least not easily or intuitively. It's not adequate to assume that people who have access to smartphones suddenly have access to everything that they need. They don't. Just because you can do something on a touch screen doesn't mean that you can handle it on a regular computer. I regularly see patrons who can send texts and use apps like Snap-Chat, but can't use Microsoft Word. Learning to code or do graphic design on a smartphone just isn't possible. People who don't have access to the internet or to computers other than a smartphone are left at a massive disadvantage.

When libraries expand our technology services beyond basic digital literacy, we are able to make quantifiable impacts in our communities. The recession of 2008 and the subsequent passage of the American Recovery and Reinvestment Act in 2009, including Broadband Technology Opportunities Program (BTOP), was a much-needed kick in the pants for libraries. Several of the chapters in this book began as BTOP-funded projects and the effects of the BTOP grants can be traced through the reports to the federal government.

During this period at Queens Library, we were able to provide over 39,000 hours of individual assistance and classroom hours and, by December 2012, had helped eighty of our patrons complete online training to qualify for industry certifications. Beyond the certifications, in my time on the BTOP team at Queens Library, I was able to observe patrons moving from learning to use the mouse, all the way up to basic HTML. I had one patron who began teaching Microsoft Office classes as a volunteer at other organizations and was able to give back to her community. Another patron who focused on our business, social media, and WordPress classes was able to start a cooking blog that provides supplemental income to her family. Those are just two of the successes I've seen myself. We also regularly received notes from patrons who had found jobs or just felt better about using computers once they finished some of our classes. In the state of Texas, BTOP-related "training efforts have reached a total of 107,466 people as of 2012." When we find out what resources best meet the needs of our communities, we can make a difference, whether it is a large impact like that of the BTOP-funded programs or smaller ones.

Now that we have identified the issue, what do we do about it? It's not only makerspaces we could be offering, although they are a convenient and visible measure of what services are available. It is frequently claimed that tens of thousands of technology industry jobs are going unfilled. What are libraries doing to ensure that our patrons have access to those jobs? Libraries can provide the bridge training necessary so that our patrons can learn to code. We have an audience for basic digital literacy classes and services, we can find ways to help push our patrons past simply using email and into truly making technology work for them. When libraries offer more involved technology programming, patrons come. From the *Library Journal* Maker Programs in Public Libraries study; "One half of public libraries say that, compared to a year ago, adult maker program attendance has increased, while 42 percent say it has stayed about the same. Only 7 percent say it has decreased. Libraries that offer coding programs have the highest percentage of increased attendance by adults." (Maker Programs in Public Libraries, 2017: 12) When they come, they are able to make use of the resources and equipment for both learning and concrete needs, "On average, one quarter of maker equipment usage (27 percent) fills a specific need for the user and is not simply exploratory. The percentages do not vary much when parsed by location or size of library" (*Maker Programs in Public Libraries*, 2017: 15).

Building equity in access to things like 3D printers and programming training is just our next logical step, and we are up to it. After all, "No other institution, public or private, does a better job of reaching people who have been left behind in today's economy, have failed to reach their potential in the city's public school system or who simply need help navigating an increasingly complex world" (Giles, 2013: 3). Libraries have the reach into the community to have a great impact on digital inclusion, not just with basic digital literacy, but to help our patrons move forward into a technology-driven world. The chapters of this book are filled with real impacts on real people, immigrants who can create and share videos with their families in their countries of origin, teenagers who learned the processes of applying for college and financial aid, even a cat whose owner was able to make it a snazzy new outfit using library resources. All of these in this book started as an idea or a response to a community need. We have the opportunity to not only make an impact on our patrons' lives, but to help them make an impact in the world. Let's get to work.

## REFERENCES

Bertot, John Carlo, Brian Real, Jean Lee, Abigail McDermott, and Paul Jaeger. *Public Libraries and Digital Inclusion*. College Park, MD: Information Policy and Access Center, 2015. Accessed October 8, 2017. http://digitalinclusion.umd.edu/sites/default/files/DigitalInclusionBrief2015.pdf.

Giles, David. *Branches of Opportunity.* New York: The Center for an Urban Future, 2013. Accessed October 8, 2017. https://nycfuture.org/pdf/Branches_of_Oppor tunity.pdf.

Horrigan, John. *Libraries 2016.* Washington, DC: Pew Research Center. Accessed October 8, 2017. http://www.pewinternet.org/2016/09/09/libraries-2016/.

*Maker Programs in Public Libraries 2017.* New York: *Library Journal,* 2017.

*Public Library Revenue, Expenditures, and Funding Sources.* Cambridge, MA: American Academy of Arts and Sciences. Accessed October 8, 2017. https://www .humanitiesindicators.org/content/indicatordoc.aspx?i=419.

# I

# IDENTIFYING THE PROBLEM

*Lauren Comito*

A series of interconnected class, economic, gender, and racial inequities has helped to create the digital divide, and there is no one solution that will close it. There are a huge range of factors that have created the differences in technology access and familiarity across classes and groups of greater or lesser privilege. By identifying the issues we can start to systematically address them. Every community will have different needs, and different libraries in those communities can use different resources, talents, and strengths to start to meet those needs, particularly when it comes to technology skills. This involves not only finding the problems but also funding the solutions. This section will address finding the money a library needs to support new programs and projects as well as providing an overview of the issues involved.

- In Fund All the Things! Erica Freudenberger breaks down the basics of grant funding. She looks at the entire process of writing for tech projects, from researching potential funders to completion and follow-up AFTER you have the money. Erica also provides insights into budgets, making the application pop, and organizing for the whole process to ensure that nothing is overlooked or lost in the complex process of applying for and administering grant funding.

# 1

## Fund All the Things

### Finding Money to Do Great Work

*Erica Freudenberger*

$\mathbf{W}$e live in a complex and disruptive world. Rather than leveling the playing field, technology has deepened systemic rifts and created the digital divide, a chasm of inequity echoing the earlier analog division of resources. This division disproportionally affects the ability of marginalized communities to accumulate social capital by denying them full participation in a technological society. The uneven distribution of resources results in disenfranchising, isolating, denying opportunity to, and socially excluding individuals and communities.

Public policy addressing the digital divide has focused primarily on providing access to technology through schools, libraries, and community organizations—but access is only the first step to creating digital equity. As Gorski (2003) points out:

> . . . this traditional understanding of the digital divide fails to capture the full picture of inequity and privilege by these gaps and the resulting educational, social, cultural, and economic ramifications, primarily for groups of people already educationally, socially, culturally, and economically oppressed. Meanwhile, such a limited view of the digital divide serves the interests of privileged groups and individuals, who can continue critiquing and working to dissolve gaps in physical access and use rates while failing to think critically and reflectively about their personal and collective roles in recycling old inequities in a new cyber form.

The digital divide reflects systemic inequities, where gaps in opportunity deny marginalized people the right to create and produce, rather than merely consume content. Communities that have unequal access to technology have fewer chances of developing capability and expertise with it and are unable to leverage technology for self-efficacy.

Public policy addressing the digital divide in the United States has focused primarily on physical access, not on policies and programs to help people develop the skills they need to navigate a digital landscape. Schools, libraries, and select community organizations were encouraged to bridge the divide by assisting communities with access issues. Public libraries empower communities not only by providing access to technology but also to training and support to create and acquire knowledge across multiple platforms, building social capital and self-efficacy. Unfortunately, public libraries are in the untenable position of having to bridge the digital divide without the allocation and support of new resources. So what's a library to do? Build a diverse funding stream, including grants, because digital equity requires resources.

## GETTING STARTED

Grant writing can be intimidating. Not for the faint of heart, it requires enthusiasm, passion, organization, and perseverance. To begin, exhale. Let go of the idea of finding money to cover the cost of operations. Prepare for rejection. Dream big. You've got this.

When putting together a proposal, keep in mind that funders want to know how a project will impact a community, not what a library needs. As Lois Gordon (L. Gordon, personal interview, October 2017) of the Mohawk Valley Library System says, it's not about the library getting a bus. It's about transporting seniors to library services in the winter and after dark, strengthening the social fabric. Talk to people in your community—not just library patrons— about what they are trying to do, find a way to help them get it done, and tie the request to the library's strategic plan. Find community stakeholders who can help make the project successful—funders prefer organizations that collaborate and, increasingly, are asking for sustainability plans for funding requests.

Successful grant writing requires preparation and organization. The first step is to establish paper and electronic files of essential, up-to-date documents, including the library's mission, vision, and values statement. Understand the library's priorities (found in the strategic plan). Is the library a 501c3? Include documentation in the folder. If not, know what type of tax-exempt status the library has, and keep that documentation. Include relevant demographic research. As statements, statuses, or demographics change, update this folder—it contains the information required by most funders.

Think about how the project proposed fits with the library's organizational capacity. Is it something the library can take on with the current staff? Does the staff have the skills and expertise to implement the project? Successful grants require a team of people with varying strengths, knowledge, and expertise. Teams may include a project coordinator, a financial wrangler, a public relations maven, and a tech nerd. The project coordinator should be familiar with project management, and if the grant requires developing technology, expertise in agile project management. Technology projects need a level of specialized knowledge—especially if there is interaction with vendors—and can get expensive quickly if not well thought out. As Carson Block (C. Block, email, February 26, 2018) points out, "The team needs its own resident geek!"

After assembling the dream team, determine what other skills and resources are needed. Funders respond favorably to collaboration, so find partners to help meet the objectives of the grant. When partnering with other organizations, establish clear objectives, expectations, and roles in the beginning, so there is no confusion once the grant is implemented. Be honest in considering the funding for the project and determine a reasonable budget that will lead to success. Create an internal communication plan to keep the library team, the community partner, and the funder on the same page.

## RESEARCH

As you begin the quest for funding, be prepared to dig in and do some research. The Foundation Directory Online database has more than 100,000 funders. If the library doesn't have access to this tool, reach out to another library, university, or community group. If that fails, use a web search engine to begin the process, and leverage your network of colleagues. Securing a grant is for the bold—be prepared to call friends who may have access to resources you don't, ask for help on social media, your board or Friends group. We live in a highly competitive funding environment, so spend time researching to ensure that you meet the needs of a funder before approaching them—you don't want to waste your time or theirs.

Once you locate a potential funder, review the organization's 990-PF form, the tax reporting form filed by federally tax-exempt organizations each year. This document allows the government and the general public to evaluate a not-for-profit and is a treasure trove of information. The website guidestar. org posts 990s, providing the mission, vision, and values statements of funders. It will also tip you off to a funder's priorities, what their limitations are (e.g., geography, type of organization, tax status), what projects have been funded in prior years, and the amount of funding awarded. Also, it identifies the officers and trustees of the organization, providing another chance to work your network. Share this information with the library board, Friends, and staff to see if anyone has connections to the potential funder. Successful grants require relationship building.

When a funder looks promising, always call before making your ask (check the protocol for applying before calling—some may not want calls, but those are the exceptions). A funder is a partner in your project, not a cash machine. When you call to discuss the project, ask about their priorities, for feedback, and whether the proposed project is a good fit. Invite the program officer or a representative to the library for a site visit to show off the library and the great work it does.

If one funder isn't interested, ask if they know another that more closely aligns with your project. Philanthropic funding is a small world—organizations communicate about the projects they fund and know what other funders prioritize. Treat the funder well, include them in the process, communicate with them throughout the project, and thank them enthusiastically and often after each time you interact and in any publicity produced to promote the project. It is the responsibility of a grant seeker to make the funder look good and to have a great experience working with you. If you do, you will find lots of opportunities for future funding.

## THE PROPOSAL

A compelling proposal demonstrates ample planning and preparation, conveys the importance of your project and its impact on the community, includes evidence of what you are capable of, documents why you are requesting funds, and demonstrates that the project is sustainable. You should be able to show a thorough understanding of the issue you're working on, be aware of who else is addressing the issue, what is being done, and the latest thinking about the topic. Follow the guidelines of the funder, and be sure that you are submitting all of the information they have requested in the format they require.

When writing the proposal, channel your inner Hemingway, and stick to clear language and simple sentences. Make a compelling argument, but stay away from flowery or unnecessary embellishments. Be clear about why you have chosen a particular funder, be specific and thorough about what the purpose of the project is and its goals and outcomes. Most importantly, be realistic—if you do not deliver what you propose (and fail to communicate with the funder along the way), you will not have a successful experience. Follow all guidelines and timelines, and include all required documentation—do not submit a proposal late and expect it to receive funding.

The goals and objectives of the project must have measurable, tangible results that positively affect your community. Identify one goal for each program in the grant. Explain how the target audience benefits from your proposal, establish a timeline to meet specific objectives and the result of each objective. Use the SMART goals framework (http://www.bpcc.edu/grants externalfunding/goalsobjectives.html) to make sure objectives are specific, measurable, attainable, relevant, and trackable. "Technology grants shouldn't be about the technology itself," wrote Carson Block (C. Block, email, February 26, 2018), "but the outcome the technology is designed to deliver. Being clear about the desired outcome (in terms lay people reading the grant can understand) can be a hurdle if the cart and horse are not oriented correctly!"

How will a funder know if the project has been successful? Identify what success looks like, and include an evaluation method in the proposal. Decide on a qualitative or quantitative measurement instrument and discuss how you will use the knowledge acquired through the grant. How will you tell the story about what you've learned? How will your community improve as a result of this project? How will the project change the way the library operates? What will the library be able to do differently going forward?

Before sending a proposal, have someone unfamiliar with the project read through and provide critical feedback. If you know someone in a development office or an experienced grant writer, ask for a review. Find out if they understand the proposal and can identify its goals and objectives, and ask how it could be improved.

## BUDGET

Unless you're a whiz with numbers, grant budgets can be tricky, so it's best to have help from the business office or someone with financial expertise. Budgets may include direct and indirect costs. Direct costs include personnel, travel, equipment, supplies, and in-kind contributions. Indirect costs are for facilities, insurance, utilities, waste management, cleaning services, and so on. Not all grants will cover indirect costs—to find out, review the funder's proposal requirements or have a conversation with the funder to clarify. Technology grants may need a specific budget indicating the cost of specific hardware, software, and licensing components.

Many funders require both a budget and a budget narrative. The budget is a spreadsheet showing how resources will be allocated. The budget narrative allows you to tell the story of how funds will be spent and help achieve the objectives of the grant. The budget narrative should explain all costs and be a realistic assessment of what is needed. Technology projects can be expensive, and cost overruns can threaten the success of a project if it isn't thoroughly planned out and assessed.

The budget should include a timeline indicating when the project will take place and when money will be spent. Check to see if the library has the same fiscal year as the funder; use the timeline to show when funds will be needed. Include information about in-kind services—including volunteer time, use of space, and professional expertise—to demonstrate that the library has skin in the game and is committed to the project. In-kind services demonstrate your wise stewardship of resources and ingenuity. Be sure to organize the budget so that it is easy to read and understand, and double-check all math. Have the library board approve the budget (and the grant) before submitting to a funder.

## COMMUNICATION

Huzzah! You've got funding! You can do all the tech things. Before beginning, let everyone know about your project and the generous partner that is making it possible. Each grant should have a communication plan with internal and external strategies.

The internal communication plan keeps the project team, management, staff, library board, and Friends of the Library on the same page. It lets everyone know what's happening when and outlines responsibilities of all parties. An internal communication plan provides an opportunity to brainstorm with a larger group about how to promote the project.

The external communication plan outlines how the library will publicize the award, where it will send press releases, what platforms it will use to market the project and the funder. Promote the funder as a partner, and include any boilerplate language required in all promotional material. Invite the funder to special events and any photo opportunities—the priority of any public relations is shining a light on the funder.

If the grant hasn't been funded, take a pause, and relax. It isn't you. The only way to secure grants is to write grants—lots and lots of grants—many of which won't be funded. As mentioned before, obtaining funding is competitive, and being passed over may not reflect on the proposal, but on limited resources. After you've had a chance to reflect, call the funder and thank them for their time, and request feedback on your proposal. Find out how it could have been improved and if it would be reconsidered with adjustments. If it's not a good fit, ask if there are other funders who may be interested in the proposal. If they do suggest another funder, ask for an introduction—remember, it's about building a relationship.

Each time a funder is approached by a library, it creates an impression not just about that organization, but the entire profession. Provide accurate information; don't skew demographic data or falsify other documentation to secure funding. Comply with the funder's process in the grant application, make sure the library's mission and vision align with the funder and respect confidentiality. Most importantly, when funded, do what the grant proposed. If there is a problem implementing the grant, communicate early and often with the funder to let them know, and suggest ways to remedy or alter the grant. Funders want projects to be successful and will do their best to make a project work. Do not surprise a funder by altering the grant without permission. If the funder decides to pull funding when the project no longer aligns with the grant proposal, be gracious. The funding world is small.

Technology is a distributive justice issue; a lack of access and facility with technology leads to a lack of opportunity, diminished access to resources, limited economic prospects, and hindered participation in the political process (Tavani, 2003). As literacy becomes increasingly entwined with technology, libraries are leveling the playing field, promoting digital equity and social justice. Libraries can work with communities to utilize digital tools for economic activities, build social capital, access services, and connect to and create knowledge. This book has inspiring examples of libraries empowering marginalized communities with technology. For many libraries—like small, rural libraries—there are real and virtual barriers in place to providing these life-changing programs. Grants can provide the resources libraries need to strengthen the social fabric in a digital age, creating knowledge, fostering collaborations, developing skills, and empowering communities to build the world—or at least their corner of it—as they would like it to be.

## ACKNOWLEDGMENT

This chapter would not have been possible without the incredible work, generosity, and teaching of Patty Wong, city librarian of the Santa Monica Public Library, who has managed to secure millions in grants to help her community thrive.

## RESOURCES

Agile Project Management: https://www.cio.com/article/3156998/agile-development/agile-project-management-a-beginners-guide.html
Elements of a Grant Proposal: http://www.hotwinds.com/Grant_Prop.html
Foundation Directory Online: http://foundationcenter.org/products/foundation-directory-online

Grant Advisor: https://grantadvisor.org/
Guide to OBE for organizations with limited resources: https://managementhelp.org/
evaluation/outcomes-evaluation-guide.htm
Guidestar: http://www.guidestar.org/Home.aspx
Outcome-Based Evaluations: https://www.imls.gov/grants/outcome-based-evaluation/
basics
Project Management Templates: http://www.projectmanagementdocs.com/
Proposal Checklist: https://www.archives.gov/nhprc/apply/evaluation-checklist.html
Purdue University's OWL on Grant Writing: https://owl.english.purdue.edu/owl/
resource/981/1/
Shaping Outcomes Course: http://www.shapingoutcomes.org/course/overview/a1.htm
SMART Goals & Objectives: http://www.bpcc.edu/grantsexternalfunding/goalsob
jectives.html

# REFERENCES

Alam, K., and S. Imran. (2015). The digital divide and social inclusion among refugee migrants. *Information Technology & People, 28*(2), 344-365. Retrieved from http://search.proquest.com.libaccess.sjlibrary.org/docview/1681459252?accountid=10361.

Gorski, P. C. (2002). Dismantling the digital divide: A multicultural education framework. *Multicultural Education, 10*(1), 28-30. Retrieved from http://search.proquest.com.libaccess.sjlibrary.org/docview/62202709?accountid=10361.

Gorski, P. C. (2003). Privilege and repression in the digital era: Rethinking the socio-politics of the digital divide. *Race, Gender & Class, 10*(4), 145. Retrieved from http://search.proquest.com.libaccess.sjlibrary.org/docview/218807872?accountid=10361.

Gregory, G. M. (2016) Moving toward digital equity. *Information Today.* 33(4), 20.

Howard, P. N., L. Busch, and P. Sheets. (2010). Comparing digital divides: Internet access and social inequality in Canada and the United States. *Canadian Journal of Communication, 35*(1), 109–128. Retrieved from http://search.proquest.com.libaccess.sjlibrary.org/docview/807511709?accountid=10361.

Kwok-Kee, W., T. Hock-Hai, C. Hock Chuan, and B. Y. Tan. (2011) Conceptualizing and testing a social cognitive model of the digital divide. *Information Systems Research*, 22(1), 170–187. doi:10.1287/isre.1090.0273.

Price-Dennis, D., and S. Carrion. (2017). Leveraging digital literacies for equity and social justice. *Language Arts, 94*(3), 190–195. Retrieved from http://search.proquest.com.libaccess.sjlibrary.org/docview/1858234991?accountid=10361.

Tavani, H. T. (2003). Ethical reflections on the digital divide. *Journal of Information, Communication & Ethics in Society, 1*(2), 99–108. Retrieved from http://search.proquest.com.libaccess.sjlibrary.org/docview/1011924111?accountid=10361.

# II

# PHYSICAL ACCESS

*Lauren Comito*

As public libraries work to create digitally literate communities, one major stumbling block they face is providing access to the physical computing equipment necessary to meet that goal. Access to and quality of library facilities can vary enormously between communities. Some communities are awash in technology and the library reflects that. Other communities have fewer assets and fewer technology, space, and general resources. This is particularly pronounced in heavily urban and rural areas, where libraries remain the main place that everyone in the community can access computers and the internet. We have tried to bridge the classic digital divide, yet in many cases our public access computers are old, slow, and have limited software options. Lack of broadband access and the resulting low connection speeds can make using the internet frustrating for patrons. Many librarians are stuck trying to maintain the systems they currently have while also ensuring access to needed updates in software with compatibility for everyone including people using the latest versions for school while also ensuring compatibility for patrons who have older iterations that they are using at home.

Finding ways to solve these issues requires creativity, and the chapters in this section show ways that librarians can look at their communities, find the barriers and needs, and figure out ways to address them. These authors show how you can bring new and more advanced equipment to your community giving access to the latest technology (or hacks getting you close to them) to everyone in the community. These chapters describe efforts to disrupt and re-create the library as space to enable the development of digital literacy skills and create space for technology access regardless of individual ability to afford it.

- Emily Scherer opened up STEAM and STEM to U.S./Mexico border populations who have low technology exposure by providing hands-on early childhood education and intergenerational learning in high poverty areas using technology.
- Alex Lent used open source software to provide laptops for patrons to use throughout the library thus opening up new spaces and working models for patrons who did not have laptops themselves.
- Ricci Yuhico created a dedicated digital space in partnership with diverse teen populations to provide an area for digital creation not just for personal expression but also to promote change in their community.

The projects in this section came from looking around the library and asking "what's missing?" or "who is missing?" then working with technology to fill that gap. The reader may want to ask themselves the same questions as they work through this section, but also ask others. What impacts should the equipment in a library have on the community? Are we using this software because it is what will work best, or because it is what we have always used? If funds are lacking, is there another solution, like open source software or furniture sitting in storage? By being creative, libraries can find new ways to improve access.

# 2

# Technology on the Border

## Bringing STEAM-Based Learning and Digital Technologies to Southern Arizona

*Emily Scherer*

Yuma is best known for its unbearable, scorching heat. Reaching temperatures upward of 120 degrees Fahrenheit in the summer, only the boldest spend much time out of doors during the day when the sun is the most relentless. The desert town attracts "snow birds" from the north each year (local lingo for northerners who spend their winters down south), their RVs littering the highways and trailer parks, metal roofs baking in the hallucinogenic heat. Nestled neatly, albeit remotely, into the far southwest corner of the state, Yuma attracts those looking to be close to the border of Mexico for various reasons—dental care, family and friends, and cheap prescriptions (doctor's note optional). Professionals are offered financial reprieves to come to Yuma and work—doctors can pay off student loans much more quickly if they're willing to journey down to the Mexican border for a year or two. The "border wall"—a metal fence built with old airstrip parts dots the landscape to the south near the communities of Somerton and San Luis. New hires for the library district are famously brought through the local farm fields on their initial tour to visit the wall; no one from the north can quite get over either the absurdity or the enormity of such a presence in southern Arizonians daily lives. Migrant workers and their families cross the border every morning for work, school, or to visit friends and family. The wall is a constant reminder that those who live in Yuma County have one foot in two very different worlds.

A large percentage of "Yumans" speak Spanish at home or grow up in bilingual homesteads; it is not unusual for children to learn English in school or, if they're lucky, in the library district's early literacy-based story times that take place at each branch several days a week. Many of the branches offer bilingual story and baby times, and several offer language programs for adults, including citizenship. I distinctly remember computer classes for adults in Spanish and English, and residents of Mexico could obtain a library card from the southernmost branch with their Mexican driver's license. One of Yuma's many strengths as a community was its focus on international services and inclusivity. There weren't many services offered in the region that didn't take into the account the area's unique vibe and cultural diversity.

In my three years as youth services manager for the Yuma County Library District, I noticed several families who attended story times with their young ones to take advantage of the opportunity for the family to learn English language skills together. It is one of my many takeaways from my time there and something that made a historic impression on me. Never again will I view story times as JUST services for children—at least in Yuma, adults occasionally learned how to speak and read in story times as well. Truly, the early literacy–based story times (particularly in language diverse communities) are family learning events.

I came to know Yuma County fairly typically—through a phone interview in the fall of 2011, during my grueling post–graduate school job search. I had obtained the last slot of their first round of phone interviews and pulled over into a rural cemetery in Wisconsin after a full day as a Teen librarian to answer their dozen or so questions. A Skype interview followed shortly after and, before I knew it, I was flying into the city's small airport to meet my future boss and youth services crew—scuttling between the county's eight libraries in a white van. Although my previous experience consisted largely of tween and teen services, the Yuma job provided an opportunity to work with young children (birth through middle school), which I greatly desired. After negotiating my salary, determining a start date, and eating my fill of steak at the local Texas Roadhouse with my future boss, I accepted the job as youth services manager for Yuma County Library District. My office was bright and full of windows; I was thrilled. I drove to Arizona from Wisconsin a few weeks later, my tiny Mini Cooper filled to the brim with clothes and knickknacks, ready to start my new venture serving Yuma County.

The library system had made it clear during the interview process that they were looking to hire someone who could bring exciting and educational programs to their library district, in addition to the already very-full schedule of events. STEAM-based learning opportunities, as well as the introductions of technology into library programs and services, were stressed as issues of importance, so I concentrated on those particular traits when planning grant opportunities for my new employer. Every year, the Yuma County Library District applied for an LSTA grant from the State of Arizona, generously funded by the Institute of Museums and Library Services. It was almost guaranteed that if you came to Yuma County Library District as a librarian or manager that at some point it would be your turn to put forth an idea. My turn came the autumn of 2013—and I already knew what I wanted to do.

During a tour of new library architecture in the Madison, Wisconsin, area several years earlier, I had stumbled upon an iPad in the back area of a youth services section just sort of hanging out, looking well-loved and worn. It had several science apps on it that children could play with and manipulate at their leisure. I perused the device, looking for library ideas, and came upon several applications I hadn't known existed—apps on insects, human anatomy, and the solar system that were both informational and fun to use. I asked the youth manager in charge about the tablet and its apps and was told it was the most popular item in the youth area—"in fact," said the manager, "children would often stop by just to 'play with the iPad'"—in other words, the device alone was bringing people into the library. I shelved the idea in the back of my brain and told myself, if ever given the budget and the space, I would make sure to include similar technologies in the youth services sections of my library. If children would enter a library to play a game or fool around on some technological device, maybe I could talk them into bringing a book home too? And why have only one? In my future library, I pictured a space with several tablets so there would be limited waiting but many opportunities to play with several different themes per library visit.

I discussed my vision with the grants manager (who was adept at turning a blasé idea into a shining one), and we began writing what would become the "Touch and Learn" project—a series of STEAM- and technology-based programs and conveniences meant to introduce children to digital technologies and all their possibilities.

Although it was 2013 and the United States, for the most part, was living in the "post-recession" world, Arizona was still hurting badly economically. In fact, some communities are still struggling with their budgets—housing sales are still lagging behind the rest of the country, and several counties and cities haven't provided raises for their employees in six years or more (Yuma County being one of them). In 2012 the current situation was dire: only 14 percent of Yuma Union High School District tenth grade students met or passed the science portions of Arizona's Instrument to Measure Standards (AIMS) test, compared to a statewide rate of 42 percent. While poverty and the bilingual nature of the Yuma community were hurdles at times that likely contributed to this rather outrageous figure, the problem went much deeper. The unemployment rate in 2012 reached a staggering 29 percent; 46 percent of households in Yuma County reported that English was not the primary language spoken in their home. While the Yuma County Library District stressed bilingual materials and programs as a priority for all eight libraries— from San Luis to Dateland—the population of the community still struggled with how best to communicate and in what language. Many families had few, if any, technological devices in their homes and oftentimes they shared what they did have. Yuma was and still is very much a community where children finish their homework assignments at the library.

The grant I spearheaded for Yuma County attempted to alleviate some of these societal issues, but like all gargantuan undertakings, it began small. The goal was simple: to launch a project in Yuma County to improve digital literacy for future educational and career success of their youth population. Community members would benefit as a whole as an educated and digitally literate youth population would eventually contribute to the overall economic and social stability of a region. As President Obama stated in his State of the Union Address (February 12, 2013): "It is vital to create classes that focus on science, technology, engineering and math—the skills today's employers are looking for to fill jobs right now and in the future." He went on to state: "Every dollar we invest in high quality early education can save more than seven dollars later on—by boosting graduation rates, reducing teen pregnancy, even reducing violent crime. In states that make it a priority to educate our youngest children . . . studies show students grow up more likely to read and do math at graduate level, graduate high school, hold a job, and form more stable families of their own." The grants manager and I took these words to heart as we put pen to paper for the Touch and Learn project and youth of Yuma County.

The Touch and Learn project's purpose was to infuse digital elements in everyday library and school programs for youth ages 5 to 12; to utilize collaboration with other agencies to improve the overall digital literacy skills of our school-aged children throughout Yuma County and usher in STEAM-based learning on a district-wide scale. The grant couldn't be everything for everyone, and it needed to start small, but its ambitions were large and encompassing from the get-go. Administration was excited about the idea and, after showing them the details in writing and getting approval, off I went to mail the application to the State of Arizona. Within a few months I received an answer: the Touch and Learn grant proposal had been accepted and awarded to the tune of nearly $25,000. The press release was prepared; the purchasing of equipment began. I felt both elated and overwhelmed.

The Touch and Learn project consisted of several parts: (1) digital evening story times with a focus on science and technology utilizing tablets with applications that expose youth and caregivers to a more diverse understanding of technological availabilities and explore their desire to read and learn, (2) a digital science station at the Main Library consisting of a tablet lab as well as iPad OPACs in the youth area for use by the general public, (3) at least two workshops for educators and caregivers on how to use some of the latest learning and STEAM-based applications available to them, and (4) a collaboration with the Cocopah Nation to provide nonfiction story times once a month at their library utilizing tables and apps.

While the collaboration with the Cocopah Nation Library was short-lived (we'll detail that later in the chapter), the opportunity arose to re-think our approach to the project because of the communication breakdown and served as a constant reminder that a project is only a good one if all the parts properly fit.

Project valuation was a large part of the grant, and staff consistently surveyed participants and collaborators for input on the effectiveness of the project—including video interviews and video shorts of the programs involved for use in social and public media outlets. Early on, the idea was to expand the program as much as possible—so much heed was paid to how people were working with the new technologies, what they appreciated about the program, and what needed to be altered. It was a constantly evolving process of re-working and learning which methods of involvement worked for our community. Bilingual applications were added to the iPads not as an afterthought but a distinct matter of priority.

The Touch and Learn grant fit with the goals and priorities of the LSTA both on the state and national levels as well as our county strategic plan. To quote the former, the goal is to: "expand services for learning and access to information and educational resources in a variety of formats, in all types of libraries, for individuals of all ages in order to support such individuals' need for education, lifelong learning, workforce development, and digital literacy skills" (https://www.imls.gov/grants/grants-state/purposes-and-priorities -lsta). We didn't feel completely off track even once; our goals were smart and in line with progressive library services; our views of good service coincided with those on the national level. Touch and Learn was both well-meaning and important in its purpose and scope.

By May of 2014, the Touch and Learn project was implemented at the Main Library in Yuma County's Youth Services Area. A recently discarded child-sized, six-person table found under a stairwell served as the basis for the initial digital science station, and the IT department quickly got to work to convert it to a ready-to-use STEAM tablet exploration site. Holes were cut, wires were run, and iPads were purchased and installed in a matter of days. An open house event (complete with press) announced the arrival of the STEAM-centered station, and it quickly became the hit of the summer at the library. IT WAS HUGE; much larger than ourselves. The news media jumped at the new excitement surrounding the library, and elementary students were interviewed on camera, exclaiming their love for their new favorite science applications. In a recent Google search, I came across a pre-made technology table—exactly like the one we constructed in Yuma County, available for a rather hefty price at one of the nation's leading library furniture companies. Our creative at-home project has garnered corporate attention and production.

While the digital science station was, and has remained in many ways, the "star of the show," less popular but equally important elements of the grant began implementation around the same time. Staff went to the Cocopah National Library after school once a month and assisted in training employees, parents, and students on how to use a tablet and find relevant applications; parents and caregivers became more attuned to applications available for students with literacy issues through night-time trainings, and our OPACs were converted to mounted tablets to complete the transition to "touch only" OPAC computers in the youth services area. In under a year, with a little help from a grant, we fully transitioned our area to one that was technologically advanced, friendly, and capable of bilingual communications (tablets are equipped to work in Spanish or English, which was a must for our community).

Disappointingly, Touch and Learn never took off at the Cocopah Nation Library. On just the second month of the Touch and Learn project there, library staff on the reservation informed us they no longer wanted to participate due to scheduling issues. The Touch and Learn program took place right after school (and shortly before the library closed) making it inconvenient for native staff to supervise. Although this was a large setback, a new partnership formed because of it with a nearby STEAM-based school. Instead of going to another library, nonfiction story times were brought to science classes. The new partnership proved to be a fruitful one—in fact, it was acknowledged that a public library setting may not be the best use for the story times and, in fact, the school setting worked much better for that portion of the program.

The digital story times programs went like this: once a month, I would lug thirty iPads complete with energetic apps and e-books to a science classroom where we could have a forty-five to sixty-minute discussion on a particular topic—like space or the solar system. Students would take turns in a classroom setting reading nonfiction books out loud, participating in games based on the topic, and engaging with apps such as "Star Walk," which allows one to consider the solar system directly above them—no matter what time of day or where they are. The location-based application was a favorite with the students and allowed them to get up, walk about, and walk the stars in their area at that particular time of day. Following the readings and games, participants engaged in a discussion of the topic and gave feedback to the county library liaison, which was usually myself and as a backup, a youth services assistant. The grant provided for a mobile cart, which allowed us to bring dozens of iPads and keep them charged in the time we were in the classroom. It was through the failure of our initial partnership that we learned that digital nonfiction story times worked in the classroom setting but not as well in the public library setting; it was also through that partnership failure of sorts that we learned what aspects of the program students liked (interaction) and those that they didn't (reading out loud in large group settings). The programs were altered based on feedback—and so Touch and Learn continued to grow and evolve to meet the various needs of its participants.

As the year wound down and Touch and Learn became part of the landscape rather than a novelty, it became clear that the implementation had been a success and that funding would have to continue for the project to continue to grow to the other branches of the library system. In 2017, several years after the first part of the process was complete, the Yuma County Library District received additional grant funding to bring science stations to two other branches in the county—both of them large Spanish-speaking communities. Somerton and San Luis welcomed their own tablet-laden tables this past year, and the program will likely continue to expand to further branches in the future.

The long-term impact of the Touch and Learn program has yet to be felt or studied, although its success clearly shows that students were ready and willing to take on a new technology challenge. The tablet OPACs worked well for nimble-fingered youth raised on touch screen technology; the science station became a premier hangout spot for the elementary aged; school-aged children were introduced to new ways of interacting with science through technologies.

I am no longer the youth services manager of Yuma County—I've moved a few hours down the road to Sierra Vista where I manage the library and teen center, but the lessons I've learned from the Touch and Learn project resonate to this day. My new library recently completed and won an LSTA grant for a mobile maker lab. And in that grant, there are stipulations for iPads, coding technologies, and computers. As I did several years before in Yuma, these items will be wheeled to underserved communities (rural areas, a nearby military installation) where technology and science will continue to be brought to school-aged children en masse via the classroom. Although in a different community now than that of Yuma (I miss the taco carts so much), the spirit of Touch and Learn continues to live on through my work and has been passed down to my colleagues who are now forming their own grants and projects that contain a similar purpose. Together, the bridge between digital access and absence is continually made a little smaller.

## REFERENCE

Obama, Barack, State of the Union Address. February 12, 2013. The Obama White House. https://obamawhitehouse.archives.gov/the-press-office/2013/02/12/remarks-president-state-union-address.

# 3

# Linux Laptops for Libraries

*Alex Lent*

In 2015 the Millis (MA) Public Library launched a fleet of entry-level laptops running the open-source operating system Ubuntu to allow patrons to have access to library technology anywhere in the building. Millis is a rural community of 8,000, located equidistant from Boston, Worcester, and Providence, the three largest cities in New England. Because it serves a population of fewer than 10,000 people, the Millis Public Library is what the American Library Association refers to as a "very small public library." The ALA could just as accurately refer to libraries of this size as "standard public libraries," because such libraries make up 60 percent of public libraries in the United States.

Among these most common-sized libraries in America, the Millis Public Library is fairly typical. It has a small staff, a small budget, and a small building. And it provides patrons with access to computers—desktop computers, organized in banks.

What makes the Millis Public Library a bit different than other libraries of its size is the fact that as of the writing of this chapter, its building is less than five years old. It is also a highly performing library, with 105,000 visits, 150,000 items circulated, 17,000 event attendees, and 15,000 computer users each year. The Millis Public Library also benefits from a hard-working staff and very dedicated trustees and volunteers who are all game to try new things in order to better serve the Millis community.

All of this is to say that while the Millis Public Library is in a new facility, is highly used, and has a great team, it is overall a very standard library. A project that succeeded in Millis—such as the project I am about to describe here—has a great chance of success elsewhere. If not in all public libraries in the United States, at least in the majority of them that the American Library Association calls "very small."

*Alex Lent*

## OBSERVATIONS LEAD TO GOALS

The Millis Public Library's desktop computers are organized in banks. These banks are located right in the middle of the Library and cannot be moved, as they require data ports and electrical outlets that are not sufficiently plentiful in other areas of the Library.

Patrons use computers in different ways. Staff had observed:

- patrons who worked quietly by themselves on computers and did not mind background noise
- patrons who worked quietly by themselves on computers and very much minded background noise
- patrons who wanted to work by themselves on computers but who needed a wide variety of one-on-one help with computers
- patrons who wanted to work collaboratively on computers together and who wanted to talk while they did so
- patrons who worked independently on computers but who wanted to be able to have conversations with their neighbors while they did so
- patrons who brought in their own devices and worked in armchairs or on couches
- patrons who brought in their own devices and worked in quiet study rooms

Staff also realized that:

- while we provided both quiet study rooms and computers, both of which are at least partly intended for students and others who need to do work, we did not provide computers in quiet study rooms
- patrons were satisfied with what the existing desktop computers could do, but patrons were not satisfied with the location of the computers and the multiple noise situations related to use of the computers
- if patrons had laptops, they could choose to work in the area of the Library that most suited their needs—whether that is near the hustle and bustle of the service desk, in a quiet study room, in an armchair or on a couch, or with other workers in a group study room.

This project also approached an issue of equality of access. Patrons who were able to bring their personal laptops into the Library—patrons who were able to afford their own laptops—were able to use technology wherever they wanted in the Library, but patrons who could not afford their own laptops were not able to use technology wherever they wanted in the Library; certain actions (laptop use) in certain areas of the Library (study rooms, comfortable chairs, etc.) were not available to certain patrons based on individual socioeconomic status. By providing laptops for patron use, we could address the socioeconomic aspect of this space issue.

From these observations and realizations, we decided to investigate the feasibility of supplementing its existing desktop computers with laptops. The main goal of this project was to allow patrons to determine where in the Library they used Library technology.

## CHOOSING THE LAPTOPS

With the main goal of the project established, it was time to look at funding. We decided to start with five laptops, after observing groups of that many students working together at our desktop computers. If we had five laptops, we could relocate groups of that size to a meeting room. We had $1,500 in our budget that could be spent on this project. That meant that we could spend as much as $300 per laptop.

Knowing that patrons were happy with their current desktop computers, we looked for laptops that were as functional and comfortable as our desktop computers and set the following technical specifications as goals:

- large screens, preferably high definition
- full keyboards with number pads
- at least four gigabytes of RAM
- at least four hours of battery life (because the Library did not intend to circulate power cords with the laptops)
- front-facing camera for video conferencing
- CD/DVD player
- at least three USB ports

We did not have strong feelings about processors because these laptops were intended to be used in the same way that the desktops were used—mostly for document creation, web browsing, and media consumption—not for resource-heavy tasks. Storage space was also not a significant consideration because patrons would not be saving items to these computers, but the Library did prefer solid-state drives over traditional hard drives with spinning discs because SSDs are more durable than HDDs.

Between these tech spec goals and the tight budget, resulting options were limited, and the Library selected the Toshiba Satellite C55. These are entry-level machines with fifteen-inch, HD screens, full keyboards, four gigs of RAM, six hours of battery life, a camera, CD/DVD players, and three USB ports. The only problem was that they had hard drives not solid-state drives. But, close enough. The Library purchased five of these laptops, for a total cost of just shy of $1,500.

## THE DECISION TO USE LINUX

We needed to find a way for the laptops to be wiped clean of changes after each use. We didn't, for example, want a patron to use a laptop and be able to access the documents saved by that laptop's previous user. And we didn't want patrons to be able to change settings or download items that could harm the computer (though we felt this would be accidental if it occurred at all).

These tasks are usually handled by a program like Deep Freeze. Computer administrators provide Deep Freeze with a computer in an ideal state, and Deep Freeze reverts the computer back to that ideal state whenever the computer is booted. So if a patron saves a document to the computer and then reboots the computer, the document will be gone when the computer starts up again.

There are two problems with Deep Freeze. The first is that it can be challenging to manage, and because the Millis Public Library has a small and very busy staff, the laptops had to be as easy to manage as possible. The second problem is that it costs money and by this point in our project, we no longer had any money—we had spent our entire project budget on the laptops.

It was at this point in this project that we decided to move away from Windows and instead use Linux. Linux is an open-source operating system that has been around in various versions for over twenty-five years. Linux is free. One of its most popular versions is Ubuntu, which is published by Canonical, Ltd. Ubuntu, like most distributions of Linux, is free. Additionally, it has a built-in feature called "Guest Session."

The Guest Session feature allows users to log into the computer as a guest. When guests log out, all the changes they have made—whether changes to settings or files saved to the computer—will have been deleted. When the next guest logs in, they log into a pristine computer. This feature accomplishes what the Library wanted Deep Freeze to accomplish and for a cost of $0. See figure 3.1.

Canonical releases new versions of Ubuntu approximately annually, with small updates more frequently. Every two years, Canonical releases a "Long-Term Support" or "LTS" version. LTS versions still need periodic small updates, but are supported by Canonical for five years. The downside of LTS versions is that they are not the cutting-edge versions that come out annually.

**Figure 3.1.  Temporary Guest Session**
Alex Lent

The Library decided to use Ubuntu 14.04 LTS for its laptops. We anticipate replacing (or repurposing, more likely) five laptops every three years, so it is likely that each wave of laptops will only ever need to have one version of Ubuntu—the laptops will be discontinued before the LTS is discontinued.

Additionally, Ubuntu is a less resource-intensive operating system than Windows—it requires less space and it requires less processing power. This means that after Ubuntu is installed, the computer will have more processing power left over to run other programs, such as browsers, than it would if it were running Windows. This is useful because it means that by using Ubuntu, we can get more power out of our entry-level laptops with their limited storage space and processing power. By using Ubuntu, we can get away with using cheap hardware.

## INSTALLING UBUNTU 14.04 LTS

This section is a walkthrough of the steps involved in installing Ubuntu.

### Step One: Download Ubuntu 14.04 LTS

Visit http://www.ubuntu.com/download/desktop and click "download." Note that you may see a decimal number after 14.04. This is the number associated with maintenance updates to LTS.

**Step Two: Create an Ubuntu install disc**
Create an install disc from the downloaded Ubuntu installer. The easiest ways to install Ubuntu are from a USB stick or from a DVD. I prefer using DVDs, because USB sticks sometimes present formatting issues that DVDs tend not to present. Learn how to do that here: https://help.ubuntu.com/community/ BurningIsoHowto.

**Step Three: Change your boot order**
Access your computer's BIOS and change the boot order so that your computer knows to start up from the install disc. Learn how to do that here: http:// www.howtogeek.com/129815/beginner-geek-how-to-change-the-boot-order -in-your-computers-bios/.

You can access the BIOS for the Toshiba Satellite by pressing F2 as soon as the red Toshiba logo appears on your screen after pressing the power button. When you have accessed the BIOS, use the keyboard to navigate until you see "Boot Order" and change the order so that CD/DVD is the first option. If you are installing from a USB drive, select "USB Drive" as the first option.

For the Toshiba, Boot Order is located under "Advanced." Select Advanced. Select "Change Boot Order." Select "ODD" (optical disc drive) and select "up" in order to move ODD to the first boot option. Press "OK. Press "Save and Exit."

Open your Optical Disc Drive and then turn off your laptop by holding the power button.

Insert your Ubuntu install disc, close the disc drive, and press the power button to turn the laptop back on.

**Step Four: Install Ubuntu**
Follow the on-screen instructions.

A menu, called the GRUB menu, should appear on your screen shortly. At this point, you can try Ubuntu without installing it or you can select "Install Ubuntu."

Select "Install Ubuntu."

The screen will go dark.

The Ubuntu logo will appear.

You'll hear computery noises.

Your cursor will appear. You can move it around, but there's nothing to click.

The screen will turn purple and a bar will appear at the top of the screen.

You'll hear a little drumroll and a window will appear.

The computery noises stop.

This all takes about three to five minutes.

The window asks you to select a language. Select the one that you'd like to use. For me, that's English.

The computery noises start again.

The window will say "Preparing to install Ubuntu" and ask if you want to install third-party software. If you say yes, you will need to select a password. I say yes and select a password. Press "continue."

Computery noises.

The window will ask how you would like to install Ubuntu. The top option is "Erase disk and install Ubuntu." This is what I recommend selecting. I leave "Encrypt the new Ubuntu installation for security" and "Use LVM with the new Ubuntu installation" unchecked. Press "Install Now."

A window will pop up saying "Write the changes to disks?" Click "continue."

It will ask where you are located. It's really asking for time zone, so if it says New York and you're in Boston, you don't need to change anything.

It will ask you to select your keyboard layout and test your keyboard. Press "continue" when you've selected the right keyboard for your needs. (I don't change anything here.)

It will ask you who you are.

Your name: I write "librarian" or "staff."

Your computer's name: I write "laptop1."

Pick a username: I use "librarian" or "staff."

Choose a password: I use the same password I set during "Preparing to install Ubuntu."

I keep "Require my password to log in" selected.

I do not select "Encrypt my home folder."

Press "continue."

A window titled "Welcome to Ubuntu" will appear and a progress bar will appear at the bottom of the window. Sit tight.

Wait.

Wait.

Wait.

Wait.

Wait.

A window will pop up that says "Installation incomplete. You need to restart the computer in order to use the new installation." Press "Restart Now." The screen will go blank. Some writing will appear. The disc drive will open. Remove the disc and close the drive.

The computer should restart.

If it doesn't restart within five minutes, hold down the power button until it turns off. Then turn the computer back on.

A blue screen may appear. No, not that one.

Wait.

The Ubuntu logo will appear.

A little drumroll sound will happen.

Then the login screen will appear.

The name you set as your username should be there, above a little box that says "Password." Enter your password in the box and press enter.

A sidebar will appear with a number of icons. A window will pop up titled "Keyboard shortcuts." Close the window.

Your installation is complete. Congratulations, you're a Linux user!

## Step Five: Hide the Grub2 menu

The following lines will hide the ugly menu that appears when you turn on the computer, which patrons do not need to see. You can skip this step if you like.

Open a terminal window and enter:

gedit /etc/default/grub

A window will open up. Modify the relevant lines to match the following:

GRUB_DEFAULT=0

GRUB_HIDDEN_TIMEOUT=0

GRUB_HIDDEN_TIMEOUT_QUIET=true

GRUB_TIMEOUT=0

Press "save" and close the window.

## Step Six: Locking the BIOS

Restart your laptop and enter your BIOS settings. Change your boot order so that HDD/SSD is the first option. This means that your computer will boot up from its hard drive, rather than from an installation disc or USB stick.

Go to the Security section of the BIOS menu and double-click "Supervisor" under BIOS password. Set a password. Save and close. This password will prevent patrons from going into your BIOS and changing your settings.

## Step Seven: Customizing the guest session

With a few easy steps, Ubuntu's Guest Session profile can be adjusted. This is appealing if you want to provide (or not provide) patrons with access to certain programs or features. The present section is a walkthrough of how the Millis Public Library customized its Guest Session profiles.

Add a new administrative user called "preferences."

Open a terminal window and enter:

sudo mkdir /etc/guest-session

It will ask you to enter your password. Do so, and press "enter":

sudo ln -s /home/preferences /etc/guest-session/skel

These lines tell the computer to make the Guest Session account look like the preferences account. Now, if you want the Guest Session to have a different desktop pattern or have some particular settings, you can make those changes in the preferences account and they'll automatically appear in the Guest Session account.

## MODIFY LIBREOFFICE TO USE MICROSOFT OFFICE FORMATS

Patrons appreciate having Microsoft Office on our desktop computers. Microsoft Office can be loaded onto Linux (most easily using PlayOnLinux, an amazing program that repackages Wine, a well-known but finicky program that allows Windows software to run on Linux). However, this is a tricky process and we needed our laptops to be as easy for staff to manage as possible so that any staff member can help patrons, rather than just one or two particularly tech-savvy staffers. Additionally, Microsoft Office, like Deep Freeze, costs money and we didn't have any.

Ubuntu comes loaded with LibreOffice, an open-source office suite. It has a program like Microsoft Word, a program like Microsoft Excel, and a program like Microsoft PowerPoint. LibreOffice looks, feels, and functions very similarly to Microsoft Office. The big worry with using LibreOffice rather than Microsoft Office is compatibility—patrons want to be able to easily save and share documents they created on LibreOffice with people who use Microsoft Office. By default, LibreOffice saves to "Open Document Format" rather than Microsoft's .doc format. When a user saves a document in LibreOffice, they can tell LibreOffice to save in Microsoft formats, but this isn't a working solution for a public library because patrons want to press save and have it work—they don't want to have to select the right format.

Fortunately, these defaults can be easily changed.

Log into the preferences account.
Open LibreOffice. In the TOOLS menu, select OPTIONS. In LOAD/
   SAVE, select GENERAL. Under "default file format and ODF set-
   tings," select a document type from the "document type" drop-down
   menu and match it with the corresponding file format in the "always
   save as" drop-down menu, as follows:
Document Type: Text Document
Always Save As: Microsoft Word 2007/2010/2013 XML
Document Type: Spreadsheet
Always Save As: Microsoft Excel 2007/2010/2013 XML
Document Type: Presentation
Always Save As: Microsoft PowerPoint 2007/2010/2013 XML

That's all it takes to make LibreOffice pretend to be Microsoft Office. I was skeptical whether these changes would stick, and I was skeptical whether these changes would really make LibreOffice fully compatible with Microsoft Office. As a test, I used LibreOffice exclusively for two weeks, writing and submitting reports, analyzing data in spreadsheets, and creating slide decks for presentations. I never ran into a single compatibility issue.

One further change you can make to LibreOffice is where documents are saved. By default, LibreOffice saves documents to the My Documents folder. Patrons sometimes have trouble locating the My Documents folder, but they almost never have trouble locating the Desktop. You can teach LibreOffice to save documents to the desktop by going into the "Tools" drop-down, selecting "Options," and selecting "Paths" under LibreOffice. Double-click "My Documents." A window will open. Click "Desktop" and then click "OK." Now when patrons save in LibreOffice, their documents will save to the desktop.

## CUSTOMIZING MOZILLA FIREFOX

Ubuntu comes loaded with Mozilla Firefox, an open-source internet browser. By tweaking its settings slightly, we can make it better serve patrons.

Open Firefox and then open "Preferences." In the "General" tab, change "When Firefox Starts:" from "Show a blank page" to "Show my homepage" and set your homepage to your library's website.

Under Downloads, click "Browse." A window will open. Click "Desktop" and then click "OK." Now when patrons download something in Firefox, it will save to the desktop, where they can easily find it.

Next, under the "Search" tab, delete all the search options besides one—having more than one option will most likely just cause frustration. I recommend using DuckDuckGo. DuckDuckGo functions a lot like Google, but it is privacy-conscious and doesn't track users' search patterns or location.

Under the "Privacy" tab, check the box labeled "Use Tracking Protection in Private Windows." Click "Manage your do-not-track settings" and make sure that the box next to "Always apply do not track" is checked. Press "OK." Under "History," select "Firefox will never remember history." We don't want patrons to be able to see what other patrons were looking at. Firefox will now need to restart.

When Firefox opens again, go to eff.org/privacybadger and follow the steps to install Privacy Badger. Privacy Badger is a little program that blocks ads that track users.

Next, go to eff.org/https-everywhere and follow the steps to install HTTPS Everywhere. The HTTP you see in front of most web addresses stands for Hypertext Transfer Protocol. It is one of the building blocks of the internet. The S in HTTPS stands for Secure. HTTPS makes your activity on the web more private by encrypting the data sent between your computer and the sites you visit. Installing HTTPS Everywhere will help protect your patrons on the internet.

### Customizing Ubuntu Search

Open "System Settings" and select "Security & Privacy." Click the "Files & Applications" tab. Uncheck all the items listed under "Include" and switch the toggle next to "Record file and application usage" to Off. Next, click the "Search" tab. Make sure that the toggle next to "Include online search results" is set to "Off." Close the window.

### Customizing the Sidebar

Close all the windows you have open and look at the sidebar on the left side of your desktop. You should see an Ubuntu icon on top, then a Firefox icon, then three LibreOffice icons, then a little shopping bag, then an Amazon logo, and then a gear logo. I recommend deleting the shopping bag—which sends you to Ubuntu's software store, the Amazon logo—which sends you to Amazon.com, and the gear icon—which sends you to "System Settings." Your patrons don't need access to any of these.

### Printing

If you have a printer at the library you'd like these laptops to be able to work with, there is an easy way to set this up. Ensure your laptop is connected to the internet and then connect it to the printer. Open "System Settings" and press "ADD." A window will appear with some information about the printer your laptop is connected to. Follow the steps on the screen to to print from a library laptop, they can bring it right up to the printer, plug in, and print.

That's it! Your operating system is ready for use.

## CIRCULATING YOUR LAPTOPS

The easiest solution we found for providing patrons with access to our laptops was to add the laptops to our catalog. We created a record for laptops and had each laptop be a title associated with that record. Their call numbers were Laptop 1 through Laptop 5 and each laptop received a barcode. We store the

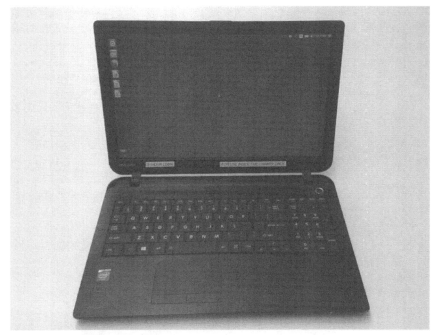

**Figure 3.2.  Configured Laptop**
Alex Lent

laptops behind the circulation desk, plugged into outlets. If a patron wants a laptop, we check the laptop out to them the same way we would check out a book to them. We gave the laptops three-hour loan periods and we do not circulate them with their power cords.

We also put stickers on the computer saying "3-Hour Loan" and "For Use Inside the Library Only." See figure 3.2.

## FINAL THOUGHTS AND FUTURE PLANS

Two years into this project, it is still going strong. These laptops have allowed us to create a more patron-focused computing ecosystem at the library. Patrons check them out and use them in comfortable chairs and on couches, in small study rooms, and in group rooms. We now have a total of fifteen laptops, which allows us to turn our multipurpose room into an ad hoc computer lab and teach computer classes or have Minecraft parties.

We considered, but ultimately decided against, providing instruction classes in the use of these laptops. The idea was that most patrons have not been exposed to Linux and might be confused. However, this has not been the case—by and large, patrons seem to be immediately able to use these laptops to do whatever they want to do. If patrons do have questions, they just bring the laptop to a staff member and ask—one of the perks of having mobile computers.

All fifteen of our laptops are holding up well—we've never had any laptops damaged or stolen and we have never even had any crashes, which cannot be said about our desktop computers. We've never had to reinstall any operating systems. We still have all fourteen of our old desktop computers, but have repurposed a few in order to open up desk space.

Our biggest challenge with our laptops is making sure that patrons know about them. We have posters, flyers, and table toppers up in strategic locations around the library and continue to remind patrons in person and through social media. Use is growing, and patrons are pleased with the option to use laptops wherever they want.

Eventually, I hope we will be able to take the next step in making library technology patron-centered and allow patrons to check out our laptops and use them outside the library for a longer period of time—perhaps as long as six months. This would allow patrons to be able to do computer-based work and homework whether the library is open or closed and no matter the patron's socioeconomic status.

# 4

## Shifting Focus toward Imminent Needs

### The Importance of Flexibility in Digital Literacy Training to Teens within the Maker Movement

*Ricci Yuhico*

To classify an age range as "digital natives" drastically oversimplifies the digital divide. For teens, especially in underserved areas, knowing social media jargon and having internet access do not automatically lead to understanding how to navigate the new norms of everyday life that necessitates digital literacy. As technology advances, it is assumed to be ubiquitous for our youth. With cheaper smartphones and data plans and increasing connectivity access in public spaces, the problem of digital access is assumed to be "resolved." Yet, any work to address a digital literacy gap should not end there.

Libraries and their staff come into play as a public access point with dedicated teen spaces and the maker movement. When library staff look to create teen spaces that can expose the youth to technology and resources for content creation, making, and remixing, the dedicated staff must also be prepared to embrace flexibility, go beyond the coding class and media production workshop, and be ready to become the emotional and knowledgeable bridge that offers training and education in the digital skills needed to fulfill many basic functions today. From applying for FAFSA or to college, or even navigating through their high school teacher's Wiki for class, teen librarians and staff must simultaneously provide a safe haven for creative expression and address these immediate informational needs.

All names of teens in this chapter have been changed or abbreviated for privacy.

### SITE BACKGROUND AND SERVICE AREA

Broward County Library's Main Library sits in the heart of Ft. Lauderdale, Florida. Opened in 1984, this flagship facility is one of 39 libraries servicing all of Broward County and is an 8-story multi-purpose building with 222,000 square feet of usable space. A branch profile of Main Library from 2013 indicates that the population of Main Library's immediate service area is approximately 270,000 but also recognizes that with its size and variety of services, users come from all over the tri-county area of Miami-Dade, Broward, and Palm Beach. Main Library is further accessible via public transit due to the proximity of the Broward Central Bus Terminal.

Known to be an architectural gem of brutalist design by Robert Gatje, the building was likened to a cracked geode by its designer, with one wall facing the Ft. Lauderdale River in keystone and the other facing the very busy Broward Boulevard in sparkling glass windows (Wallman, 2014). Hurricane Wilma devastated the library in 2005; it then underwent a seemingly endless construction that spanned nine years and caused door counts to drop off almost by 50 percent.

Since the new millennium, gentrification of Downtown Ft. Lauderdale has become much stronger and much more readily apparent. In this area, during the time of segregation and prior to the creation of Main Library, blacks of Ft. Lauderdale were forced to live west of the railroad tracks alongside Andrews Avenue and along NE 6th Avenue, now named Sistrunk Boulevard for Dr. James Sistrunk, the first black doctor in Broward County who helped establish the first black hospital for the area in the 1930s. Today, while the Sistrunk Corridor is still the epicenter of and home to Ft. Lauderdale's black community, Downtown Ft. Lauderdale is quickly becoming a "predominantly white enclave" (Dimattei, 2013).

Perhaps noted as a renaissance and a transformation of the neighborhood into a walkable, play/live/work area, now with monthly last-Saturday Art Walks and microbreweries, the Downtown Ft. Lauderdale scene has gained the urban art scene stamp of approval, according to the *Broward Palm Beach New Times* (Tracy, 2014).

Though he described the area as somewhere he would "hesitate" to drive through at nighttime, founder of what is now known as FATVillage (Flagler. Arts. Technology.) Doug McGraw purchased properties in Downtown Ft. Lauderdale in 1999 (Tracy, 2014). In a comprehensive analysis of Broward County Library services by MGT of America, Inc., just 17 years ago when McGraw purchased properties in the area, data showed that median income housing levels surrounding the Main Library and extending west along the Sistrunk Corridor just under 3 miles toward the African-American Research Library and Cultural Center (AARLC) was between $16,180 and $28,068 (Li and Storey, 2011). Closer to the water, moving just a bit east of Main Library and east from the railroad tracks on Andrews Avenue, the difference

**Table 4.1.  Data of the most recent U.S. Census Bureau aggregated by Cubit Planning Inc.'s Income by Zipcode website. Zip codes in the table are within Main Library's immediate service area and where the majority of teen users for this project live, as discussed further in the chapter.**

| Zip Code | Median Household Income (Inflation adjusted dollars, American Community Survey 2015, 5-year estimates) |
| --- | --- |
| 33311 | $31,913 |
| 33301 | $76,345 |
| 33304 | $50,732 |
| 33312 | $48,913 |
| 33313 | $34,151 |

"Income by Zip," Cubit Planning, Inc. Accessed June 2017.

was jarring; median incomes of households jumped up to as high as $126,572 (Li and Storey, 2011).

Just 10 years later, the monthly Art Walk began in FATVillage where artists' galleries, studios, and other creative businesses hold open houses for the public. Yet, despite the arrival of such a renowned event and new focus of the urban arts scene and culture, the income disparity of Downtown Ft. Lauderdale continues to remain unaddressed, as shown in table 4.1 (https://www.incomebyzipcode.com/florida).

According to Census data and estimates for 2015, nearly 90 percent of the 63,000 individuals living in the 33311 zip code are black; in the neighboring zip codes of 33301 and 33304, nearly 80 percent of the 14,000 and nearly 82 percent of the 17,000 residents are white, respectively. This demonstrates, as with other cases of gentrification, that merely rebranding an area to build up its livability does not necessarily uplift those in lower income areas. In examining this community profile, it's important to note that Pew Research indicates that households with lower incomes and racial minorities are less likely to have broadband access at home; when non-broadband users were asked why they did not have access, they stated that the monthly fee was just too much (Horrigan & Duggan, 2015). In 2015 surveyed non-adopters also recognize that not having access puts them at a "major disadvantage of some sort" (Horrigan & Duggan, 2015). Maintaining access to thriving public spaces like libraries that offer informal learning environments and digital access for those individuals who do not feel the benefits of an injection of wealth becomes that much more necessary.

The immediate service area of Downtown Ft. Lauderdale has included sharp differences in median household incomes over many years now. With Broward Boulevard and Sistrunk Boulevard and Andrews Avenue akin to racial and socioeconomic lines of demarcation, youth within the underserved areas of Downtown Ft. Lauderdale live in a completely different world than those in the richer areas. Ironically, and painfully, are they welcome in an area that they were born into due to the entrenched history of racism?

In 2009, with the "renaissance" that continued to invigorate Downtown Ft. Lauderdale, Main Library began to increase its access to technology with a public internet computer station facility, dubbed the Cybrary, on its seventh floor and access to 72 public-use computers. By 2012 a Cyber Commons computer lab on the first floor also opened with over 56 public-use computers. After the creation of a "DIY" committee of library staff and leadership, it was decided that Main Library, with its flagship status, space capacity, and wide service area, and finally the wrap-up of construction and repair from Hurricane Wilma, would be the site to host new spaces that would incorporate the maker movement and new cutting-edge technology classes into library services. This would eventually include The Studio, a digital arts space just for teens.

## Problem Analysis

Main Library, however much it continues to be an architectural gem with an advantageous square footage that was certainly sufficient for the wide and varied service area that the library hoped to provide access to, did not have a dedicated teen area. A branch profile of Main Library indicates that it serves a total of 19 schools, including: 6 public elementary schools; 1 public middle school; 1 public high school; 2 alternative high schools, Whiddon Rogers and Seagull Alternative; 6 upper and lower private schools; Broward Virtual School; Florida Virtual School; and Broward Homeschool Association. Further analysis revealed that 2 high schools are within 2 miles of the Library: Stranahan and Ft. Lauderdale High. In December 2015 I was hired as the Teen librarian and broadened the scope of contact to include additional schools within a 5-mile radius: Mavericks High of Central Broward and St. Thomas Aquinas High School.

Even with 5 local high schools within the immediate service area, no fully realized dedicated teen spaces that incorporated digital media access or informal digital learning in the neighboring branches of Main Library existed in the area of Downtown Ft. Lauderdale. Shelving for the young adult collection was pushed to the back corner of the children's department and programs for them were shuffled from floor to floor based on availability. The kind of service provided seemed to be an afterthought; an accommodation made and pieced together with the resources allotted and shared with the Youth Services department, lacking any events pertaining to digital media/literacy classes or input, direction and engagement from teens. In reexamining how we could better provide services based on twenty-first century needs and aligning that with best practices from YALSA, practices at the Main Library left a gaping hole in resources (Professional Values Task Force of the YALSA, "Core Professional Values for the Teen Services Profession," 2015).

At the time, teen services as a whole were being restructured across the system (SLJ, "Teen Services Positions at Risk at Broward County Library," 2015). With the task of expanding hours across the system without an increase in funding, organizational charts were proposed without teen librarians to allow for more generalization of service by professional staff. The job titles and organizational chart removed "Youth" and "Teen" designations that, though library leadership maintained those services would not leave, had previously guaranteed focus of professional staff through the 40 branches of system.

## PROJECT SUMMARY

Under the direction of new leadership, Broward County Library began reevaluating how the system could continue its transformation into a library that better provided services suited toward twenty-first century needs. Main Library, equipped with underutilized square footage, the advantage of the proximity to the Broward Central Bus Terminal, and a broad service area in the burgeoning city center, was a building that would be reenvisioned to provide a wide range of services—and eventually house a dedicated teen space equipped with technology, with plans for creative digital media programs and workshops and room to grow.

An abbreviated timeline is as follows:

- 2012—the very first Do-It-Yourself (DIY) Committee was formed in order to study creative spaces for the Main Library, including an iteration for space dedicated to teen services. Library leadership visited teen spaces such as YOUmedia Miami in the Miami-Dade Public Library System, Broward's neighboring large urban library system.
- 2013—Broward County Public Library Foundation awarded Broward County Library, under the direction of a new library director, Skye Patrick, the DIY Grant for $400,000 to make plans from the committee a reality.
- December 2013—Broward County Library soft launched its flagship makerspace, the Creation Station, in the main library, occupying an empty space in the second floor, a lab for all ages emphasizing the democratization of information, equipped with 3D printers and digital media production classes.

- January 2014—Broward County Library hired its Digital Initiatives coordinator; a second DIY committee was formed to analyze remainder of grant money for creative spaces and opportunities to expand services.
- Early 2015—written draft plans began for a teen-dedicated space in Main Library.
- December 2015—hiring of a librarian dedicated to teen services.

In the first iteration of plans in 2015, the teen space would occupy a room on the first floor of Main Library with floor to ceiling glass windows, full of a mix of flexible furniture, and computers, a sound booth, and some shelving. After plans were submitted and initial furniture purchased, however, the project stalled for roughly a year due to attrition and lack of dedicated, focused staff.

At the start of my work in Broward County Libraries in December 2015 as a librarian, Senior dedicated to teen services, my primary directive was to lead and shape the teen space in the library to include creative digital classes involving media production, following the precedent and success set by the launch of the Creation Station. Expenditure from the DIY grant had left a remaining $200,000 for the creation of a teen space and another possible creative-space area down the line.

## PROCESS

A digital native cannot be assumed to be all-knowing, especially with varying levels of access. To assume that an age range simply knows the answers because they were born in a year when technology is apparently ubiquitous to those who can have it is fraught with complications. If one assumes that teens already "know" technology, they would be surprised to see that teens are still enthusiastic about a tech-oriented space of their own. In this space, teens would have access to programs and classes centered around digital media production classes, similar to that of the Creation Station.

The DIY Team had been calling the project the "Teen Tech Studio," which was subsequently shortened to The Studio. To be able to execute the project, further foundations had to be laid down prior to the soft opening of The Studio. Much of the groundwork to get a functioning digital arts space running had little to do with setting up digital media classes.

The groundwork aligned with YALSA best practices for teen services: There needed to be inclusion of teen input in space design and program offerings, and having an almost blank slate was a perfect opportunity for soliciting current teen volunteers' engagement. A handful of teens was registered as volunteers at the beginning of my employment, and a Teen Advisory Board (TAB) had been set up but had not met in quite some time due to attrition of staff. Main Library also needed to establish its reputation as a facility for teens among other youth-serving nonprofits, governmental organizations, and the local high schools. With Main Library's downtown location, surrounded by government and office buildings rather than neighborhoods, teen services in the building were minimal at best, with no dedicated area or service point. Teens had not been asked for their input on how they saw the future of what our offerings could be at the library. Programs were shifted from floor to floor based on availability and the collection itself was shelved in a far corner away from most of the children's materials. The four computers designated for youth, ages 12 to 19, were in an open floor area, available for general internet access, but did not have the software installed or hardware capabilities to engage in digital media classes.

One key input from the teens was related to the placement of their dedicated space. With the YA collection overcrowded into a dimly lit corner of the second floor next to the Juvenile fiction, I sought a solution that would allow room for the collection to breathe and make it a more accessible and engaging display for the materials. During this time, our Adult Reference Services section supervisor was in the midst of creating a more dynamic Main Library and left 108 bays vacant on the third floor as collections were shifted. The shelving space was more than adequate for spreading out the YA fiction according to appropriate shelving standards and left room for growth. Enlisting the help of our teen volunteers, the materials were moved from the second floor to the third floor. In an effort to make the area more inclusive of teen opinions and to provide teen ownership of the area, chalkboard vinyl stickers were added to the bookcase end caps that they could redecorate every month.

Original plans for The Studio had been drafted prior to my arrival, with most of the pieces of furniture already purchased. These were a mix of modular and nesting chairs and fewer mobile, larger pieces. With the bulk of the furniture inside the space, arranged according to the layout, the first meeting of the TAB took place in this first floor area. During the meeting, while the 10 teens recognized the beauty of the natural light and tall ceilings of the room, they ultimately did not want to be a focal point for any individuals entering the library or using the public space adjacent to it.

An opportunity presented itself where The Studio's floorplan could be relocated to the third floor of the facility in an unused storage space adjacent to where the YA collection was now housed. This provided for the increased privacy for attending teens that was requested at the TAB meeting; it also allowed for a sense of ownership for teen volunteers who were involved in moving the collection and demonstrated that library staff were

**Table 4.2.** Requisitions were filed for all of these items and most, especially the peripherals pertaining to video/photo and audio/music, were filled prior to and after the soft launch.

| Item | Audio/Music | Software |
|---|---|---|
| iMac (27inch) | USB microphones | Adobe Creative Suite |
| Projector | Live vocal microphones | Final Cut Pro X |
| **Video/Photo** | Tripod microphone stand | Compressor |
| DSLRs | Audio interface | Motion 5 |
| Shotgun On-Camera Mic | 88-key USB MIDI | **Design** |
| GoPro Hero Black (Action cameras) | keyboard controller | Drawing tablet |
| Fluid head tripod | Portable Grand Piano | Scanner |
| Muslin backdrops with light set | On Stage Classic Single-X | |
| 3-light mini-boom kit | keyboard stand | |
| Chromakey green 3-panel frame | Music sheet stands | |
| | Sony headphones | |

sincerely willing to take their opinions and needs into consideration. The proposal was approved by library leadership soon after. An abbreviated list of hardware and software for the initial purchase is in table 4.2 with hardware divided into its corresponding purpose.

By May 2016 storage in the third floor unused space was redistributed throughout the building and throughout the library system. Furniture, unopened desktops, a staff computer, and a door frame were in place for a soft opening of The Studio. By June 1, 2016, Main Library would have its digital arts space for teens.

Reflecting on previous work in YOUmedia Miami, I was able to borrow from those experiences and deep-dive into the outline that was already in place in Broward County Library. As part of the original cohort of the YOUmedia Network, each learning lab, including Miami's, used principles from the Connected Learning pedagogy and was designed with an "overarching purpose to create a space that supported digital and traditional literacy development and was welcoming of, engaging to, and easily accessible by teens" (Larson et al., 2017). As defined by the Connected Learning Alliance, housed by the Digital Media and Learning Research Hub and supported as part of the MacArthur Foundation's Digital Media and Learning Initiative, Connected Learning is "when someone is pursuing a personal interest with the support of peers, mentors and caring adults, and in ways that open up opportunities for them" (https://clalliance.org/why-connected-learning/).

The methodology posits that the most resilient kind of learning is one that is interest- and user-driven and is encouraged with external support of mentors and peers. It is contingent on the staff who are designing teen digital media spaces that the environment (including staff, floor plan, resources) is open and encouraging enough for teens to feel open to any number of possibilities that they wish to pursue—be it something that they had not yet considered or a lifelong dream. It is important to note as well that an informal learning environment does not assume any prior knowledge of the user and allows youth to engage with the space at their own pace and intensity. With the experiences of the teens of The Studio, from a young lady experimenting with the green screen and pretending to be on the weather channel in post-production in iMovie, to David and John using the Canon T5 and the lighting kits to level up from phone selfies to learning how to take artistic headshots, it was evident that this environment was achieved.

To ensure continuity and sustainability, an Operations Manual was written, which included what I had dubbed the "Cardinal Rules" of the space: "Respect for *all individuals* makes this place possible" and "Feel free to be and express yourself!" (Yuhico, "The Studio Operations Manual," December 2016). By introducing each and every teen who walked into The Studio to its overarching premise, the possibilities and workshops that they could learn from, and to the rules, an environment was provided for them to experiment and tinker with less fear of judgment. The Operations Manual also included: opening and closing procedures, daily procedures, library card usage, media releases for teen users for social media and data capturing, media storage for student projects, purchasing procedures, volunteer vetting procedures for adults and teens, vendor booking, weekly schedule procedures, facilities/ maintenance requests, and emergency guidelines.

From February to March 2016, The Studio was presented to the DIY committee and to the funders, the Broward County Public Library Foundation. It was formally introduced as ". . . the premiere digital arts studio at the Library for young adults, ages 14–19, in the Downtown Ft. Lauderdale area and Broward County . . . free and open to registered teens so that they can have access to new technology." It was emphasized that the space be "open, accessible, and accommodating space for teens to learn sans requirements and grading scales" and that users would be encouraged to "pursue their own interests and become creators of unique content and digital art." While their learned skills in digital media production could be as simple as "providing an artistic outlet," ultimately these skills would empower them to "creatively respond" to the issues that they care about. It was also proposed to the DIY committee and to the funders that: "A curriculum of workshops and programs will be implemented but will remain flexible to accommodate the needs of participants, who will be encouraged to pursue their own interests, thereby defining, developing, and then refining the activities in The Studio" (Yuhico, 2016).

Keeping in mind the pedagogical framework and the community analysis, I outlined some measurable goals: achieving 100 registrants by December

2016 and reaching teens across the county, but having the most impact in Downtown Ft. Lauderdale to bring exposure to teens who may not have tech access. Qualitative goals were contingent on my informal observations and the inclusion of a survey that I was unable to execute prior to my resignation from the post, yet I hoped to see "marked improvement" in digital literacy through group and point-of-service instruction to teens by the staff, media production skills, social skills and community awareness, and the perception of the library as a place of learning and community (Yuhico, "The [Teen Tech] Studio," January 2016).

## RESULTS, LESSONS LEARNED, AND STORIES

Until December, programs in the space included film production, music production, graphic design, game design, and photography and were facilitated by staff, presenters, and volunteers who ultimately took on the role of mentors.

Weekly schedules with tentative digital workshops and programs and staffing concerns were sent to Youth Services staff and Main Library leadership. As noted in an overview report of the soft opening between June and October 2016 emailed to library administration, I wrote that "many [teens] come into The Studio with their own agenda"—as noted in the following cases (Yuhico, "The Studio Soft Opening Review," 2016). Once teens were encouraged to come into this environment, where a heavy emphasis was placed on respect, access to technology, encouragement to pursue their goals (whatever they may be), and trust, they were then ready to utilize the space as they deemed fit, shaping the experiences and offerings of The Studio, as intended. It was imperative to me that any cross-trained staff must be mindful that teens will have their own goals to accomplish and that thoughtful program ideas planned, even with their input, may be shirked in lieu of homework or other imminent needs.

The soft launch of The Studio was an overall success. In the Arts & Science district in Downtown Ft. Lauderdale, teens now have a space, regardless of socioeconomic background, to engage in the "renaissance" of the area.

Between June 1 and December 2, 2016, 230 teens were exposed to this informal learning environment full of maker activities, digital media production tech, and safe space for engagement and collaboration, well beyond the initial goal of 100. Of the aggregated statistics, between June and October, The Studio had a door count of over 200 teens a month, not including any class or nonprofit visits, with repeat visitors frequenting the space and utilizing the resources there (Yuhico, 2016). The influx and reliability of repeat visitors

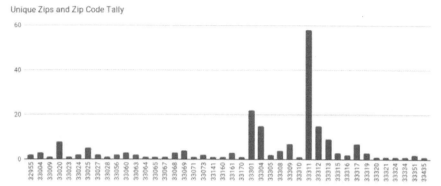

**Figure 4.1.** Zip code tallies demonstrating that teens from the targeted service area saw the most attendance in The Studio.

demonstrated the viability of The Studio and reinforced the intentional ownership of the space by the teens. At one point, Ana, a then rising sophomore, peered at her younger sister through the glass wall and made teasing faces at her, sneering "You can't come in, you're too young!"

Upon entering The Studio, teens were asked if they would provide their name, age, and zip code for statistical capturing; though they were not required to provide all of the information, 133 of them did. Zip code tallies demonstrated that the targeting of the service area for young adults was successful and that the area saw the most attendance in the space. See figure 4.1.

According to Drew Davidson of Carnegie Mellon, with just the exposure to possibilities and hanging out (within the framework of Connected Learning), a teen's awareness of the things that they *could* do just gets raised (Toppo, 2011). With 58 teens living in 33311 where the median household income is $31,913, it is my hope the research stands true through the test of time. In several instances, it happened before my eyes in The Studio.

Billy, 17, had been one of the very first volunteers when I first started in my position at the Main Library; though The Studio itself was not opened yet, he was one of the few teen volunteers who provided feedback on which floor it should be on and how the end caps of the bookshelves should look. He continued to come to Main Library as he saw the progress of The Studio and, when it opened, was one of its frequent users. One of Billy's hobbies was drawing cartoon figures and creating backstories for each original character. When I introduced him to the Wacom tablet and suggested that he try to color in his pieces digitally and begin saving them to a cloud-based server to make sure he didn't lose his art, his interest piqued. Prior to entering The Studio, though he had already uploaded his analog artwork on Instagram via his phone, he had not used an iMac or drawing tablet. Through one-on-one assistance, I taught him how to use the drawing tablet and with additional help from a volunteer, he learned how to use the brush tool on Photoshop to color in his characters and brought each to life. He continually showed me a new character each time he got bored and told me winding stories—that had so many twists and turns (often comically violent and tragic) that I eventually taught him how to use a Plot Diagram and how to take notes on his characters and their complex backstories. Eventually, Billy began to arrive with detailed profiles on his characters. I floated once the idea of webcomics to him; the next day, he stated that, rather than comics, he wanted to create a mash-up of a story-card game with his characters.

One evening, he asked for help at one of the available desktops. On this occasion, the Wacom tablet was put aside and on the computer was the Florida DMV homepage. Billy asked me how to navigate through the page to be sure he was definitely taking the correct driver's exam and receiving credit for it. Then, he asked if I could "help" him take his exam; I laughed and told him that he ought to be sure he passed on his own merits because he'd soon be driving on the road with me. It was an interesting juxtaposition to witness; Billy, by all intents and purposes, had become proficient in navigating a trade software for designers and artists, but still requested point-of-service help on a government website. Though I did not ask why he came to take the exam in a public forum, I had confirmed previously that he did not have access to a printer at home. At the time of his first entry into The Studio, Billy confirmed that he lived in the neighboring zip code 33311.

Since 2005, Pew Research has noted that of all the age demographics, teens are the creators of original content online more than any other bracket (Lenhart et al., 2007). Now, with the saturation of mobile devices, any social media app can make nearly all teen smartphone users content creators in a heartbeat (provided with data connectivity). A 2015 Pew Research survey found that nearly three-quarters of teens have or have access to a smartphone; of the remainder, 30 percent have access to a basic phone and 12 percent have no cell phone of any type (Lenhart, 2015). In Billy's example, even with smartphone access and a level up in content creation via Photoshop, I still became a bridge to "necessary" life tracks that are now only accessible online.

With regard to "traditional" life tracks toward adulthood, Brian in particular needed consistent guidance. In order to complete his community service requirement to graduate high school, Brian began volunteering at Main Library around the same time that Billy started. A rapport had been established with Brian, and he had always expressed an eagerness to help at the library and to provide feedback for teen services. With continued encouragement from me and my colleagues, he was able to finish his senior year at Whiddon Rogers Education Center and proudly walked into the library with his high school diploma to show to us. Yet, the next step in his journey involved an uncharted path for him and his family; he expressed that, though he eventually wanted to apply to Broward Community College after a semester off, he did not know how or if he could afford it. After consistent asking and perhaps unwarranted discipline on my end (though emotional labor can be another chapter altogether), Brian finally was ready to apply to Broward Community College. He simply did not know, however, where to begin. Amid the loud and dynamic atmosphere of The Studio, I sat with him, navigated him to the school website, and brought him to the application form. With formatting of text and calls to family to verify information, he completed the form by the end of the day; I ensured that the email address he put in was one that he remembered and would be able to check fairly frequently and reminded him that his email would be the primary point of contact between him and the school. He then saw on his student portal that FAFSA information was needed. Once again, with some nettling, a few days later, we began one-on-one going through his FAFSA application. Due to the scope of the application and the necessity of personal information, the form took much longer to finish. When he initially had to return to the FAFSA form that had saved his progress, he was unaware of how to navigate back to his portal. Like Billy, Brian had participated in a number of digital production activities and was proficient in using the Canon T5i, uploading the pictures to the computer, and even working with them in Photoshop. Yet, it was truly a proud moment for him to finish both of these college-bound steps and be accepted for his first semester by Spring 2017.

If one can argue that perhaps there are other college- and career-related guidance resources that are offered for the youth, how do we also address when classroom teachers continue to incorporate tech and content of their own into their curriculums? Teens must also have an access point for their class resources and learn to navigate their own teacher's digital footprint. For Lisa, a new freshman who had not yet experienced a hard academic year and was enrolled in her very first Advanced Placement class in Human Geography, it was imperative that she follow her teacher's instructions. Her teacher had uploaded all chapters and worksheets onto a website that upon navigating was found to be quite bulky. Unlike the ease she felt navigating through social media, the site created by her teacher was initially indiscernible; chapters and assignments could not be located without going through multiple links. When the semester first began, Lisa needed focused one-on-one assistance to print the items needed for her homework assignments. When she was unable to highlight certain texts due to a script error, I instructed her on how to screenshot material. Though Lisa routinely engaged in maker activities in the designated craft zone of The Studio and learned to be more comfortable with

Mac OS, her informational needs at those moments required the librarian that could help her with an unwieldy course website.

Teens who come in that need assistance in the topics or skills that had been discussed previously or would be discussed at an upcoming date further demonstrate the necessity of continuously shifting staff behavior toward their needs as the learners and users of the space. The open forum of The Studio also allowed for teens to pursue their interests at their own pace, sometimes taking them to advanced projects that needed volunteer reinforcement and more research on my end. One teen in particular, James, continues to use The Studio to create content for his YouTube channel, pursuing his dreams of being a writer, actor, film director, and editor. By utilizing the DSLRs, Sony 4K camera, The Studio's subscription to the Adobe Creative Cloud, tools he did not have at home at the time, coupled with one-on-one guidance and his own "strive" each time he entered The Studio, James created numerous videos and continues to build upon his online brand and digital portfolio. His capacity to learn and untraditional schedule with his alternative high school often required high levels of attention outside scheduled workshop times (though he was always eager to look at the whiteboard and see what he could glean from the week). In the near future, I hope that staff that have succeeded my position in The Studio examine his digital literacy needs and demonstrate ways to create invoices for his eventual commissioned work.

Even with teens supposedly hyperconnected and more relentless in creating a digital footprint, and an inclination toward creative activities once exposed to them, what I found in several attending teens was also the constant need for assistance in the more "pragmatic" matters of digital literacy. What we have known to be "*online* banking" or "filling out a job application *online*"—teens are not faced with any other alternatives. It is not an *online form*—it is simply the only form readily available. There is no other realistic or convenient way to fill out the FAFSA or a community college application or even fill out an online résumé form that differed from the format of one that they worked so hard on with their teacher or with me. These are the norms that youth are facing today, regardless of access. To ignore their access to tech, leave unexamined the underlying socioeconomic effects in their lives, and see them simply as digital natives because of their age range does not address their hierarchy of needs in any deeper or meaningful way and does them an overall disservice. Even in the midst of the maker movement, even with examining how to bring creative tech to their lives so they can address the issues that matter to them, teens still need instruction in, dare I say, "traditional" forms of digital literacy that have been so ingrained in everyday life. When constructing teen spaces, build in, as much as one can, the capacity to be flexible and provide one-on-one instruction to teens that need solutions to the pragmatic side of digital literacy.

In Main Library, The Studio's attendance continues to grow and new faces show eagerness and excitement for a digital space of their own. A Virtual Tour of The Studio can be found via: https://accutour.com/virtualtour/thestudio/.

## REFERENCES

Dimattei, Christine, "Fort Lauderdale Neighborhood Has Change of Heart in Sistrunk Naming Debate," *WLRN* (Miami, FL), Oct. 21, 2013. http://wlrn.org/post/fort -lauderdale-neighborhood-has-change-heart-sistrunk-naming-debate

Horrigan, John, and Maeve Duggan, *"Home Broadband 2015: The share of Americans with broadband at home has plateaued, and more rely only on their smartphones for online access,"* Dec. 21, 2015. Accessed June 2017. www.pewinternet .org/2015/12/21/home-broadband-2015/.

Larson, Kiley, Mizuko Ito, Eric Brown, Mike Hawkins, Nichole Pinkard, and Penny Sebring, "Safe Space and Shared Interests." 2013. Accessed June 2017. https:// clalliance.org/publications/safe-space-and-shared-interests-youmedia-chicago-as -a-laboratory-for-connected-learning/.

Li, Linus, and John Storey, "A Comprehensive Analysis of the Broward County Libraries Division's Public Library Services," (final report to Broward County Libraries Division, Ft. Lauderdale, FL, Feb. 11, 2011). www.miamidade.gov/ mayor/library/Service-Model-Working-Group/SM08%20Other%20Comparisons/ SM8%20Other%20Comparisons%20%20Attachments/Broward%20County%20 Libraries%20Final%20Report.pdf.

Lenhart, Amanda, Mary Madden, Aaron Smith, and Alexandra MacGill, "Teens and Social Media," *PEW Research*, Dec. 19, 2007. Accessed July 2017. www.pewin ternet.org/2007/12/19/teens-and-social-media/

Lenhart, Amanda, "Teens, Social Media & Technology Overview 2015," *PEW Research,* April 9, 2015. Accessed July 2017. www.pewinternet.org/2015/04/09 /teens-social-media-technology-2015/.

Professional Values Task Force of the YALSA, "Core Professional Values for the Teen Services Profession," June 27, 2015. Accessed June 2017. www.ala.org/ yalsa/core-professional-values-teen-services-profession.

SLJ, "Teen Services Positions at Risk at Broward County Library," Dec. 3, 2015. Accessed May 2017. www.slj.com/2015/12/public-libraries/teen-services-positions -at-risk-at-broward-county-library/.

Toppo, Greg, "Digital Library Aims to Expand Kids' Media Literacy," *USA Today* (Chicago, IL), Oct. 10, 2011. https://usatoday30.usatoday.com/news/education /story/2011-10-09/chicago-teens-build-media-literacy-in-digital-library/50714312/1.

Tracy, Liz, "How Flagler Village Became Fort Lauderdale's Cultural Core," *Broward Palm Beach New Times* (Broward County, FL), Nov. 25, 2014. www.broward

palmbeach.com/music/how-flagler-village-became-fort-lauderdales-cultural-core
-6436114.

Wallman, Brittany, "Broward Main Library fully open after nine years of construction," *Sun Sentinel* (Broward County, FL), Dec. 13, 2014. www.sun-sentinel.com
/local/broward/fl-broward-main-library-20141212-story.html.

Yuhico, Ricci, "The [Teen Tech] Studio," (unpublished report for administrators, Broward County Library, January 2016).

Yuhico, Ricci, "The Studio Operations Manual," (unpublished report for administrators, Broward County Library, December 2016).

Yuhico, Ricci, "The Studio Soft Opening Review," (unpublished report for administrators, Broward County Library, 2016).

# TRAINING

*Lauren Comito*

Once patrons have access to the physical technology equipment, they need training to develop modern digital literacy skills. Giving patrons access to tech tools without training opportunities only increases the perception of barriers to entry. Without some initial support patrons with low exposure to technology will just have the sentiment that "some people get it and some people don't" reinforced. Giving patrons training and the tools to understand and play with new technology empowers them to not only use technology outside of the library but to be open to the exploration and play that are essential to being comfortable with tech. In many cases, it's not only the patrons who need training; it is the library staff as well. After all, it is difficult to teach concepts and programs that you do not know yourself. So training for staff in new technologies and the basics of things like IT and web literacy is also necessary.

While technology training has been happening in libraries for as long as there has been technology in libraries, new approaches to new problems are starting to emerge. Library professionals are moving beyond the basic "here is how you use work/Excel/email so you can get a job" course structure. Library computer training focuses on results-based learning where there are clear objectives and aims to provide users with the deeper skills needed for using technology for entrepreneurial, design, and creative purposes.

This chapter is focused on libraries using technology training for community engagement and empowerment. This is tech training taken past resumes and email and into deeper engagement, allowing individuals to leverage technology for individual and community self-reliance. Training can provide a bridge over the digital divide for library patrons. This chapter will cover ways in which technology training can be offered in underserved communities.

- Davis Erin Anderson describes a "train the trainer" model to spread web literacy throughout the library profession and thus allowing those staff to teach the concepts in the communities they serve.
- Block, Fisher, and Stokes created a library model where staff at small libraries could train to be their own IT and tech support using a combination of practical hands-on and online training.
- Salt Lake City Public Library crowdsourced tech training by creating a cadre of volunteers who went out into libraries and the larger community to provide training, classes, and technology exposure to the public at large with the specific charge of empowering their community through technology.

# 5

## Cracking the Code

### The IMLS / Mozilla Web Literacy for Library Staff Project

*Davis Erin Anderson*

**A** 2016 study from the UN's International Telecommunications Union determined that 47 percent of the world's population uses the internet, a number that has grown in the months since (Taylor, 2016). The explosion of what is a relatively new technology has created myriad challenges: Our closely held personal information has become more vulnerable, our media environment has irrevocably shifted, and industry has changed to accommodate a networked society. As core elements of our operations move to an online environment, knowing how to successfully create, share, and learn on the web has quickly become a basic foundational skill, alongside the three Rs (reading, writing, and arithmetic). For the 47 percent of the world who are online and the millions more who will join them, building a basic understanding of the internet as a system and the web as a communications protocol has become a key element for engaging with the day-to-day business of life.

Libraries have been witness to these technological shifts. As described throughout this book, they have been at the forefront of ensuring the continued adaptation of our communities to a networked way of life. Along the way, opportunities for partnerships have emerged. This chapter will discuss the efforts of the Mozilla Foundation, in concert with the Institute of Museum and Library Services, The Technology and Social Change Group at the University of Washington Information School, and library partners across the United States, to provide learners with a better understanding of the functionality and culture of the web. The following pages detail the experience of Metropolitan New York Library Council (METRO), one of the pilot sites, and will review the outcomes of METRO's work as well as the overall Web Literacy Skills for Library Staff project.

## DEVELOPING THE WEB LITERACY MAP

In 2013 Mozilla Foundation staff and volunteers began to create a skills-based framework to meet the diverse needs of existing and new audiences on the web. To create a sustainable model to fill this need, Mozilla embarked on background research that included focus groups and interviews with the following stakeholders: teachers, web and technology experts, scientists, afterschool leaders, and community members (Chung, "Web Literacy 2.0"). This research included a review of past Mozilla field research in Bangladesh, Kenya, India, and Chicago, Illinois, as well as an environmental scan of extant standards for teaching web skills, including the American Library Association's Digital Literacy definition (Chung, Gill). Results from these efforts indicated that any new model must be approachable to learners of all levels and accessible to diverse audiences, including those whose socioeconomic backgrounds have prevented them from joining the early adopters online. In addition, the web literacy framework must provide avenues for audiences to develop a deep skill set; it must be applicable to learners anywhere in their journey.

After diligent investigation, the team at Mozilla developed the Web Literacy Map, a set of competencies and activities designed to help people read, write, and participate effectively online. These three skills comprise the foundation of the Mozilla framework and are defined as follows:

- "Read" explores the critical skills involved in exploring the web. This category includes activities that help learners understand how information moves through the web, how to find and navigate this information, and how to evaluate web content for accuracy and truthfulness. This category comprises four elements: Evaluate, Synthesize, Navigate, and Search. Each element includes a set of competencies and activities that can be found online at https://learning.mozilla.org/en-US/web-literacy/read/.
- "Write" explores how the web is built. This category includes activities that help learners understand how to create content online, whether through extant tools or by beginning to code, and the protocols for remixing extant online content to create something new. This category is composed of five elements: Design, Code, Compose, Revise, and Remix. Each element includes a set of competencies and activities that can be found online at https://learning.mozilla.org/en-US/web-literacy/write/.
- "Participate" explores how to connect with others on the web. This category includes activities that help learners understand how to create and foster healthy communities online through working in the open, respecting copyright, and protecting oneself online. This category encompasses five elements: Connect, Protect, Open Practice, Contribute, and Share. Each

element includes a set of competencies and activities that can be found online at https://learning.mozilla.org/en-US/web-literacy/participate/.

Mozilla's Web Literacy Map is displayed as a circle, reinforcing the notion that these skills are interdependent and cumulative. Online audiences can find the complete Web Literacy Map at https://learning.mozilla.org/en-US /web-literacy/. The map's interface is interactive; selecting one of fourteen skills leads web users to a page detailing the competencies and activities for each one. In many cases, the curriculum in the Web Literacy Map applies to more than one skill. This provides educators with an opportunity to create a complete lesson plan drawing on multiple activities. Moreover, as described by Mozilla's executive director Mark Furman and senior lead Meghan McDermott, these activities provide offline opportunities for those in low-income communities, often in developing countries, to understand the impact of using the web even if they have yet to go online themselves. See figure 5.1.

The Web Literacy Map aligns with twenty-first century leadership skills like problem solving, communication, creativity, and collaboration. Each of the fourteen Web Literacy Skills maps to at least one twenty-first century skill, as depicted by the bands of colors emanating from each slice of the Web Literacy Map.

# Web Literacy

A framework for entry-level web literacy & 21st Century skills. Explore the map by selecting what you want to learn more about, to see definitions and activities.

21st Century Skills

☑ **Problem-Solving**

☑ **Communication**

☑ **Creativity**

☐ **Collaboration**

**Figure 5.1.**
Mozilla Interactive Web Literacy Map, rev. 2016, available at https://learning.mozilla.org/en-US/web-literacy

## THE WEB LITERACY SKILLS FOR LIBRARY STAFF PROGRAM

Recognizing that libraries are deeply invested in teaching technology skills to the public, Mozilla worked with the Technology and Social Change Group (TASCHA) at the University of Washington Information School to successfully apply for an Institute of Museum and Library Services (IMLS) Laura Bush 21st Century Librarian Program Grant. The Web Literacy Skills for Library Staff was awarded $808,601; as stated on the IMLS website, the project sought to:

1. Adapt and refine Mozilla's Web Literacy skills, curriculum, tools, and resources for public library staff and pilot in five public library systems and one library school of information;
2. Connect and convey these core web literacy skills with digital badges; and
3. Develop a strategy for scalability to other public libraries across the country (RE-00-15-0105-15).

The project launched in January 2016 with an advisory council meeting that included representatives of IMLS, Mozilla, and library leaders from around the country (Mozilla Foundation Staff, "Project Kickoff"). At this meeting challenges surfaced in allocating staff time, empowering library staff to gain new or otherwise update their skills, engaging unionized workers, and navigating the decentralized nature of library systems. Nevertheless, the group agreed that the project provided abundant opportunities in creating space for librarians to gain expertise at crafting Web Literacy education, equipping often under-resourced departments with high-quality and open resources for further skill development, and tapping into or otherwise providing enhanced credentialing to learners. Advisory council members elected to participate in one of three subcommittees: pilot selection, evaluation, and scale/sustainability.

The project selection subcommittee planned an application process to identify five public library systems across the United States, ensuring a diverse pool of institutions, with regard to geography and demographics. Each applicant was asked to provide a narrative of their capacity for taking on the Web Literacy Skills for Library Staff project, a project plan, ideas for future work, and a budget narrative. Selected institutions ultimately included five public library systems and two consortia. Each site was awarded $10,000 for their work on the pilot project:

- Anythink Libraries, Colorado
- Cleveland Public Library, Cleveland, Ohio

- Central New York Library Council (CLRC), Upstate New York
- Metropolitan New York Library Council (METRO), New York, New York
- Multnomah County Library, Oregon
- Providence Public Library, Providence, Rhode Island
- Toledo-Lucas County Public Library, Toledo, Ohio

Additionally, an application process was put in place to secure a school of information studies that would test and review curriculum, training, and credentials for library school students. The University of Washington iSchool was selected to join the program as a representative of library and information science degree programs.

Project participants from the pilot sites met for the first time in Chicago, Illinois, on June 7, 2016, for a kickoff meeting (Chung, "Mozilla IMLS Web Literacy for Library Staff Pilots Kick-Off Meeting"). The gathering included an introduction to the project, a train-the-trainer session on the activities in the Web Literacy Map, and planning time for future work on the project. The group experienced elements of Mozilla's Web Literacy curriculum as learners, with the goal of enhancing their own toolkits for eventually leading events of their own. Meeting facilitators shared several activities developed by Mozilla, including Perform the Net, where the group was separated into small teams and asked to develop a model to explain the mechanics of the web using pipe cleaners, modeling clay, Lego characters, and other objects. Other activities included Werewolf in the Middle (a game-of-Telephone-like game explaining security vulnerabilities on the web) and Spectrogram (a human-sized rating scale that provides space for discussion around Web Literacy topics). These activities featured a few of the web-based tools Mozilla offers, including Thimble, WebMaker, and X-ray Goggles.

As an immediate outcome of the kickoff meeting in Chicago, Mozilla staff planned an expanded daylong training on the Web Literacy curriculum for additional library staff (Chung, "Web Literacy Train-the-Trainer Workshop for Libraries"). This event attracted over seventy-five participants to Cleveland Public Library's central branch from all seven pilot institutions, though the number of representatives from each library varied considerably. The event featured an in-depth review of Web Literacy curriculum and demonstrated how a longer training might take shape. With a deeper dive into the available curriculum, including the introduction of activities like HTML Puzzle Boxes, Tag Tag Revolution, Web Literacy Bingo, and CSS blocks, pilot sites had the opportunity to further develop their training plans ("Web Literacy Skills for Library Staff Agenda").

In addition to these in-person meetings, pilot sites kept in touch via a series of community calls. Scheduled on a monthly basis, these calls provided time for each site to share the progress made on their projects and ask questions of one another. Mozilla staff were available for consultations on an as-needed basis, and check-ins were scheduled with each pilot site as well. The pilots were also called upon to share their perceptions of this project in two phone interviews with TASCHA's assessment team.

Initially scheduled to run for a six-month term, the Mozilla Web Literacy Skills for Library Staff project was extended for another six months in order to develop and test a badging platform. Designed by the UK–based charity Digitalme, the badging interface provides pilot sites with a mechanism for motivating and engaging learners around Web Literacy subjects while demonstrating skill acquisition to potential employers. Open Badge Academy, Digitalme's system, provides one badge for each of the fourteen in the Web Literacy map. The system is designed to allow facilitators to remix Mozilla's suite of badges, ultimately allowing the badging system to accommodate newly developed curriculum and providing additional use cases for digital badging. As of this writing, six of the seven initial pilot sites are testing the badging system within their training environments.

## Training New York City and Westchester County Library Staff

One of nine regional library councils blanketing New York State, METRO's geographical coverage includes New York City and Westchester County. The Web Literacy for Library Staff project afforded METRO an excellent opportunity to work with the four public library systems in their membership: Brooklyn Public Library (BPL), Queens Library, The New York Public Library (NYPL), and Westchester Library System (WLS).

As one of the two consortia-based pilot sites working on the Web Literacy Skills for Library Staff program, METRO opted to adopt a train-the-trainers approach to sharing Mozilla's framework with library staff. The pilot program was offered at two locations: METRO's Training Center in central Manhattan in August/September 2016 and in Westchester County in October/November 2016. A small project team was established for the duration of METRO's work on the first phase of this project. The team included Danilo Campos, technical director for Social Impact at GitHub; Allison Midgley, technology trainer at WLS; and the author of this chapter. Using Mozilla's Web Literacy map, the project team helped create curriculum for and lead the trainings.

Each of the four partner locations was asked for their preference regarding participant selection. BPL, Queens Library, and NYPL extended invitations to between eight and ten staff members for a total of twenty-eight participants. While our immediate audience was composed of library staff, it was important to METRO to ultimately provide resources to all of New York's residents, irrespective of their socioeconomic status. We worked with senior staff at each system on outreach and recruitment for these workshops. This way, we could ensure that librarians at branch libraries had equal access to our trainings and could therefore bring these new teaching tools to their patrons.

The majority of participants selected for the NYC-based workshops had prior experience providing training and other programming around technology skills, and so Mozilla's Web Literacy Framework was taught as an addition to their already-extensive toolkits. Westchester County, meanwhile, opted to open these trainings to any interested library staff. Participants came from several areas within the library, and these trainings provided them with ideas for how to integrate Web Literacy activities into programs already on offer.

The framework for both runs of workshops followed the triptych of skills found within the Web Literacy Map: Read, Write, and Participate. Each skill was covered in a three-hour workshop, for a total of nine hours of training time overall. The initial goal for these workshops was to touch on each of the fourteen skills included in the map, but this was quickly determined to be untenable given the sheer amount of information that could be covered in a thorough exploration of the map. Activities were selected from those demonstrated at the in-person training programs provided by Mozilla, and the session was enhanced with training time to cover any topics addressed within the activities themselves.

The agenda for the first run of these workshops is provided below; minor adjustments were made to the version offered at Westchester. Specific instructions for the activities listed can be found at https://learning.mozilla .org/en-US/activities. In addition to working through Web Literacy activities or demonstrating concepts contained therein, two forms of assessment were developed for each session: one tested participants' understanding of content after the session was completed, and the other asked for feedback on the activities themselves.

### Workshop One: Read

*Workshop outcomes:*

- Participants will understand the way information moves around the internet
- Participants will understand how and why to evaluate information on the web

*Agenda:*

*Welcome*
Introduce facilitators and the project; answer questions.

*Web Literacy Bingo*
Ask learners to explore the meaning of and concepts included in the Web
Literacy Map with a five-by-five "bingo card."

*Spectrogram*
Set the stage for group discussion by asking learners to stand on a human-
sized rating scale based on how much they agree with web-literacy
related statements.

*Perform the Net*
After discussing how the internet works and watching a video on packets,
use pipe cleaners, string, small fuzzy balls, and other materials to create
a model of the internet with a small group.

[Break]

*Large group discussion*
Share and discuss the ways in which our three library systems are currently
teaching technology to their patrons.

*Kraken the Code*
Discuss methods for discerning truth from fiction in our online media. Use
a worksheet to understand how websites talk about the Kraken.

*Assessment & Closing*
Answer any last questions; ask learners to spend some reflective time to
share their input on the day's activities.


### Workshop Two: Write

*Workshop outcomes:*

- At the end of this workshop, participants will understand the basics of
  HTML tags
- At the end of this workshop, participants will know what CSS is and how
  it fits together with HTML


*Agenda:*

*Welcome*
Review the agenda for the day and answer any questions.

*Networking*
Pair up to discuss challenges and opportunities in teaching Web Literacy skills based on prompts from the facilitators.

*Overview of HTML*
Using a text document, demonstrate HTML.

*Tag Tag Revolution*
In this offline activity, help learners understand how HTML tags operate.

[Break]

*Explore Thimble and X-ray Goggles*
Get to know Mozilla's tools with a couple of fun websites.

*Overview of CSS*
Demonstrate CSS and how it interacts with HTML.

*CSS Building Blocks*
Provide unstructured time for learners to position and style colorful boxes on a webpage using CSS while learning about coding, composing, designing.

*Who Am I?*
Conduct a reverse image search to find information about a subject online; revise a webpage with new text and images.

*Assessment & Closing*
Answer any last questions; ask learners to spend some reflective time to share their input on the day's activities.

### Workshop Three: Participate

*Workshop outcomes:*

- Understand the meaning of openness on the web
- Start a conversation about staying safe on the web

*Agenda*

*Welcome*
Review the agenda for the day and answer any questions.

*HTML Cubes*
Help learners understand how to nest tags appropriately.

*Overview of copyright/fair use on the web*
Discuss copyright and fair use and their applicability to web content. Review how to best located content for reuse online.

*Fair Use Free-for-all*
Remix a webpage with new images; share with a partner.

[Break]

*Hack the News*
Use X-ray Goggles to remix a news website.

*Small group discussion*
Break into small groups to discuss how the activities can be used in your work.

*Spectrogram*
Review our progress by re-running the spectrogram on our comfort with Web Literacy.

*Assessment & Closing*
Answer any last questions; ask learners to spend some reflective time to share their input on the day's activities.

After running these workshops at both METRO and WLS, it became clear that a pre-session survey would have benefitted this workshop. First, both cohorts contained a wide range of levels of exposure to the content in question; some students had a deep understanding of the content covered, while others were learning concepts like HTML and CSS for the first time. Assessment records show that a portion of participants felt that facilitators worked too quickly through technical aspects of the activities. In addition, facilitators could have done a better job at expressing the design challenge inherent in remixing Mozilla's activities for an audience of adults. Our goal in the workshop was to explore how Mozilla's activities could be re-purposed for an audience of staff members, yet comments in the assessment showed that our workshops seemed to be geared toward YA librarians who run programs.

The project leads also captured feedback on Mozilla's curriculum. By and large, participants felt that the activities have a lot to offer, though the discrete nature of each activity posed a challenge to building an overarching curriculum. For the code-based activities in particular, it was a struggle to fill the gap between offline activities and those that required exploration of code. The assessment module took a tally of the number of participants who expressed willingness to continue to develop remixes of Mozilla's curriculum; of the nineteen participants at the first session at METRO, eight were interested in creating remixes of the activities they saw.

## Pilot Program Outcomes

TASCHA released their assessment of Mozilla's Web Literacy for Library Staff project in June 2016 (Fellows et al.). The report gives a history of the project, describes the evaluation approach used to review the project, and shares an assessment of the pilot sites' experience with the program. As mentioned above, feedback from each pilot site was collected in two separate hour-long phone calls. In addition, METRO shared the results of their assessment modules with the project evaluators.

Across the 8 pilot sites, almost 300 library staff members and 1 library school student (via an independent study) were trained using Mozilla's Web Literacy tools. The number of individuals trained at the pilot libraries ranged from 8 to 140, with a median of 20 (METRO's workshops reach 36 participants total). As detailed in TASCHA's report, nearly all of the pilot sites were able to meet their goals for number of staff trained.

Pilot sites were given latitude to decide their approach in sharing Web Literacy programming with library staff. Ultimately, two training methods were employed: train-the-trainer, in which skills were taught to one group with the expectation that group members would then teach others, and the cohort trainings approach where information was shared with end users directly. METRO was one of four pilot sites that worked in a train-the-trainer format. Others included Anythink Libraries, Cleveland Public Library, and CLRC. Within this set, variations emerged in:

- Localizing the training materials
- Offering trainings to member libraries
- Creating new curriculum for intranet-hosted training materials

Providence Public Library, Toledo-Lucas County Public Library, and the University of Washington iSchool opted to create cohort-based trainings with small groups of library staff.

Across the pilot sites, expectations varied as to whether these trainings were mandatory for all staff. The most elective of these pilots came from UW, which included the curriculum within a nonrequired course on a fully elective basis. Meanwhile Anythink held a requirement that all staff attend TechFest, their annual training event, at which Web Literacy activities were featured. Pilot sites were evenly split in their election to provide training to only credentialed libraries or to the entirety of library staff. (METRO's trainings fell into the latter category.)

TASCHA's review includes an overview of the effects of these trainings on participants. Across the 8 pilot locations, participants expressed that they both enjoyed and benefitted from the Web Literacy trainings. A limited amount of negative feedback came from individuals who felt these topics were not relevant to their work. Principal outcomes for participants included increased confidence in using technology, learning new skills, expressing an interest in developing a more advanced skill set, and feeling more prepared to assist with patron inquiries. For the pilot sites in aggregate, outcomes included the opportunity to innovate on previously developed professional development programs, improving IT services, and the opportunity to provide leadership in this area. A major challenge remains in continuing this work: the opportunity costs necessary to commit to continuous Web Literacy training.

## ONGOING WORK

In Phase II of this project, which culminated in late 2017, pilot sites continue to provide Web Literacy training to their staff while testing and sharing feed-back on Open Badge Academy. To support this work, each pilot site engaged in a series of one-on-one video calls with Digitalme to explore the capabilities of Open Badge Academy. Pilot sites are working to remix extant badges from Mozilla and created new badges to support related concepts.

TASCHA's assessment revealed that many pilot sites, METRO included, were looking for more of a through line between Web Literacy activities. Mozilla's curriculum developer has since started to address this; after an in-depth review, Mozilla has engaged members of their Web Literacy Leaders in designing a pathway for teaching these activities that are suitable for both in-person cohorts and individuals learning about Web Literacy in an asynchronous, online basis. Additionally, Mozilla created a set of videos featuring explanations of the Web Literacy activities as well as background concepts explored in each one. The tutorials can be made available within Open Badge Academy to create a self-directed experience for learners. Currently available only to pilot sites, these videos were to be made public in late 2017.

METRO's work with Mozilla's Web Literacy for Library Staff led to a new partnership with the Brooklyn Public Library, New York Public Library, and Queens Library. A project titled NYC Digital Safety: Privacy & Security will train frontline library staff critical components of protecting online information. Supported by the City of New York, and with input from Data & Society, the New America Foundation, Library Freedom Project, and Mozilla Foundation, the project will position libraries to assist over 250,000 residents throughout the five boroughs with their questions and concerns around digital privacy and data security. The program will make use of training materials developed by Data Privacy Project, Library Freedom Project, and, of course, Mozilla Foundation.

## REFERENCES

Chung, An-Me. "Mozilla IMLS Web Literacy for Library Staff Pilots Kick-Off Meeting," Mozilla Learning. June 23, 2016. https://learning.mozilla.org/blog/mozilla-imls-web-literacy-for-library-staff-pilots-kick-off-meeting.

Chung, An-Me. "Web Literacy Skills for Library Staff: Web Literacy Train-the-Trainer Workshop for Libraries," Read, Write, Participate. September 21, 2016. https://medium.com/read-write-participate/web-literacy-skills-for-library-staff-e86f6140facc.

Chung, An-Me, and Iris Bond Gill. "What Web Literacy Skills Are Missing from Learning Standards?" Read, Write, Participate. https://medium.com/read-write-participate/what-essential-web-skills-are-missing-from-current-learning-standards-66e1b6e99c72.

Chung, An-Me, Iris Bond Gill, and Ian O'Byrne. "Web Literacy 2.0." https://mozilla.github.io/content/web-lit-whitepaper/.

Fellows, Michelle, Katie Davis, and Cadi Russell-Sauve. "Learning and Leading: An Evaluation of the Digital Skills for Digital Librarians Project." June 2016.

Mozilla Foundation Staff. "Project Kickoff: Web Literacy Skills for Library Staff," IMLS UpNext Blog. February 4, 2016. https://www.imls.gov/news-events/upnext-blog/2016/02/project-kickoff-web-literacy-skills-library-staff.

Surman, Mark, and Meghan McDermott. "We're Not Teaching the Web Correctly," The Brookings Institute. https://www.brookings.edu/wp-content/uploads/2017/07/meaningful-education-times-uncertainty-essay-13-surman-mcdermott.pdf.

Taylor, Adam. "47 Percent of the World's Population Now Use the Internet, Study Says," *Washington Post*. November 22, 2016. https;//www.washingtonpost.com/news/worldviews/wp/2016/11/22/47-percent-of-the-worlds-population-now-use-the-internet-users-study-says.

"Web Literacy Skills for Library Staff Agenda," ThimbleProjects.org. https://thimbleprojects.org/chadsansing/92359/#step-1.

# 6

## You Can Do I.T.

### Raising Tech Confidence and Competencies in Rural Texas

*Carson Block, Cindy Fisher, and Henry Stokes*

In two years, the You Can Do I.T. program from the Texas State Library and Archives Commission (TSLAC) transformed technological literacy among library workers in rural Texas. The hands-on classes held throughout the state turned those challenged by technology into confident masters, giving nontechnologists a firm grasp of the foundational concepts and vocabulary to harness the technology that they use to support patrons. Now also offered as a free online curriculum, anyone can access the engaging and straightforward resources that shed light on the technological mysteries of everyday library technology.

### DESCRIPTION OF PROBLEM

It's often said that "Everything is bigger in Texas," and the digital divide is no exception in the Lone Star State. CompTIA reports that the majority of tech sector jobs in Texas are all clustered around the big urban areas of Dallas, Austin, San Antonio, and Houston.

Outside these metroplexes, within the huge, rural expanse of one of the nation's largest states, you'll find a dearth of broadband deployment and technology expertise. This means Texas's small, rural communities are less likely to have access to high-speed internet and the services it enables. This means fewer training and job opportunities and less support for small business entrepreneurship, causing these communities to suffer economically. Studies show that communities with broadband access are also healthier, and those that are more digitally isolated have more poor health outcomes with higher rates of chronic illnesses like obesity and diabetes. And a lack

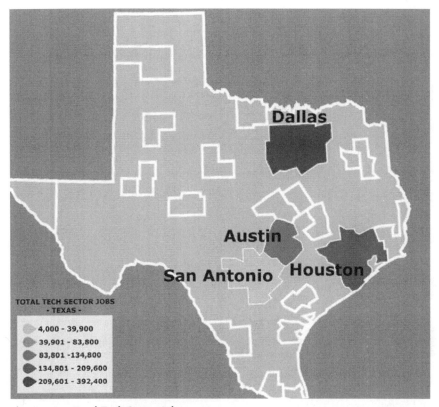

**Figure 6.1.   Total Tech Sector Jobs**
Metro Area (2016)

of broadband-enabled e-government services makes for less-informed citizens, setting up communities for failure. So, what can be done to make a Texas-sized bridge, connecting the state's rural communities to the same levels of success in the digital world as their urban counterparts?

Enter the public library. Small, rural libraries can act as the all-important access point to economic growth and life-saving services. Often the only source for free WiFi in the community, stories abound of patrons situating themselves in their local library's parking lot after hours utilizing the library's internet to perform their daily tasks.

Besides the high-speed internet access, staff at these libraries can provide much-needed digital literacy programs so the community knows how to use the technology, thus helping to ferry their community across their own bridge. But the bridge itself is made of Ethernet cables, CPUs, access points, print management software, and firewalls. It is built of I.T. And like all bridges, it is susceptible to erosion and disrepair, requiring continual maintenance and improvements. Staff in libraries must be stewards of their bridges, capable of keeping them standing strong into the future. But how can staff at small rural libraries obtain the basic skills to act as these stewards to preserve and sustain their infrastructure and thereby narrow the digital divide for their communities?

We faced this dilemma in a big way in Texas. Prior to 2012 Texas had ten fully staffed regional public library systems across the whole state, with most systems having continuing education consultants of their own, in addition to these at the Texas State Library and Archives Commission (TSLAC). With federal funding from the Library Services and Technology Act (LSTA), the State Library was able to provide the Technical Assistance Negotiated Grant (TANG) program to the regional systems. TANG enabled the systems to hire Information Technology (IT) Consultants who would provide I.T. support for individual libraries, both in-person and remotely, in their respective regions. The staff person's technical expertise was utilized for a variety of needs, such as keeping public access computers up and running and installing new hardware and software. A few provided training, but it was mostly direct on-site support. TANG was widely held to be one of the most popular and beloved programs that TSLAC provided.

In 2012 the Texas State Legislature's biennial budget reduced state funding for the State Library by 64 percent and cut state funding for the agency's library programs by 88 percent. The State Library had to lay off 20 workers and eliminate several long-running library programs. As a result of the legislature's action, TSLAC was unable to meet its federal maintenance of effort requirements for LSTA support from the Institute of Museum and Library Services (IMLS), which resulted in a loss of $900,000 in LSTA funding. LSTA was the sole funding source for the state's regional library systems and the TANG program, which provided the technical expertise. A loss of this magnitude meant that a primary source of technical help for Texas's public libraries to maintain their public access computers and networks was eliminated. Additionally, their access to technology training and skill development via Continuing Education (CE) programs (now reduced to a single TSLAC Technology Consultant) was severely limited.

In 2013 TSLAC distributed an I.T. Support Survey, asking Texas public libraries to rate how well they felt their current I.T. support was working, now that the systems and TANG consultants were no longer a resource. Respondents were asked if they had used the TANG program, how they were currently handling I.T. support, how well they felt their current support arrangements were working, and about areas where they felt they needed the most training and assistance.

The majority of respondents provided ratings of Good or Very Well, about a third rated support as fair, and 12 percent rated their support as Poor or Very

Poor. The data indicated that libraries who were serving smaller populations ("small libraries") were more likely to be dissatisfied (in the Poor/Very Poor category) with their I.T. support. A correlation was found between size and the use of contractors or volunteers. Smaller libraries reported utilizing these outside sources more often, whereas larger libraries were more likely to have gotten support from within their city or county or to have full-time staff dedicated to I.T. support. Survey results indicated that, ideally, libraries would have good city/county I.T. support or knowledgeable, reliable volunteers or contract vendors. But many libraries, particularly small rural ones, reported that they did not have consistent access to higher levels of support. Analysis of the data indicated that the more access a library had to technology savvy staff and support, the higher their satisfaction with I.T. services. In other words, libraries do better when staff can do I.T. themselves.

At the time of the survey, staff at TSLAC noted that essential library competencies, such as those outlined in WebJunction's Competency Index for the Library Field, included a variety of *basic I.T. skills*, in addition to traditional library skills. Working at a library means you should have some basic I.T. skills. The survey's results showed how important it was to provide statewide training opportunities in core library technology and troubleshooting skills, particularly for small, rural libraries, as these areas are essential to providing basic library services and maintaining satisfactory I.T. support.

The survey results encouraged TSLAC to explore the goal of enhancing basic I.T. support competencies in library staff by offering a self-paced, online Basic Library I.T. Support Skills suite of courses, enhanced by face-to-face, hands-on training offerings around the state. The contractor would be asked to conduct an in-person workshop series first, so they could then be recorded and the footage incorporated into the online course.

What does I.T. in libraries actually look like? It largely involves the management of multiple public access computers and their supporting networks for use by patrons and staff. The workshop series would focus on these related skills.

A previously designed curriculum from former TANG consultant Mack Skinner for a four-day "Computer Technologist" certification program was used as the model for the new, streamlined workshop. It was determined that the workshop should be one day in length as technology topics are best presented in training as smaller, more easily digestible chunks. The single day made it easier for library staff to commit time and resources to attend. To cover the range of content involved with managing public access computers, the workshop was split into two separate years. The first year's series would focus on networking basics (routers, WiFi, cabling, broadband, etc.), and the following year's series would focus on hardware/software basics (parts, functions, updates, purchasing, etc.), with both highlighting security and the importance of backups.

## OBJECTIVES FOR WORKSHOP SERIES
## NETWORKING AND HARDWARE/SOFTWARE

### Section I: Network hardware, cabling and internet service providers (ISP)

Workshop participants will be able to:

- Define common terms used in computer networking
- Understand broadband options available and find ISPs serving their library and/or community
- Demonstrate the ability to conduct speed checks to monitor broadband service in their library
- Identify hardware devices used/needed in a computer network
- Understand the functions and/or purpose of common network devices
- Understand modern cabling design and specifications, and best practices to use when installing network cabling
- Understand the basic concepts of the TCP/IP protocol
- Understand simple IP address and subnet mask examples
- Understand the basic requirements for configuring TCP/IP network clients

### Section II: Computer hardware

Workshop participants will be able to:

- Recognize and explain the function of external parts of a standard desktop and laptop
- Recognize and explain the function of the various ports and cables
- Recognize and explain the function of the internal parts of a standard desktop and laptop
- Understand and evaluate computer specifications (chip types, memory, speed, storage, 32- vs 64-bit)
- Define important hardware terms
- Demonstrate ability to do basic maintenance (for instance cleaning, adding memory, replacing basic components)
- Find reliable sources for reviews and purchasing

## Section III: Networking configuration and security skills

Workshop participants will be able to:

- Understand the basics of wireless networking protocols and security
- Log in and configure a typical wired and wireless router
- Configure a router for internet access
- Connect computers to form a peer-to-peer wireless network
- Use networking utilities to analyze, diagnose, and document networks
- Demonstrate the ability to configure segmented public/staff library networks for security
- Understand drive mapping concepts and map a network drive
- Implement basic backups, security, and restoration procedures

## Section IV: Software and Security

Workshop participants will be able to:

- Understand the basics of BIOS security (settings, passwords)
- Describe the function of the operating system
- Understand the function of device drivers, install printers
- Demonstrate ability to update operating system, drivers, etc.
- Understand importance of and proper use of antivirus, anti-malware, and other security software
- Evaluate public access computer systems such as time and printer management (Insight, and system restoration software such as DeepFreeze, Clean Slate, Drive Vaccine, etc.)
- Implement basic backups, security, and restoration procedures

## Workshop Branding

The entire workshop series was given the name: "You Can Do I.T.!" (YCDI.T.) and used the famous World War II inspirational poster of Rosie the Riveter as part of its branding. She was given TSLAC agency colors of blue and red, and with her strong, flexing arm held up, seen to be holding in her fist an Ethernet cable in an empowering way. Later, she would be considered the official mascot of the program and was dubbed "I.T. Heidi." An action figure was even made and taken on the road to be photographed with participants (in the manner of a garden gnome).

The inspirational "Rosie the Riveter" image originally highlighted the powerful role of women working during wartime. With the I.T. field considered a traditionally male-dominated space, with librarianship considered traditionally female—it was possible to draw a comparison to World War II. The aim of the You Can Do I.T.! program was to inspire library staff to feel more confident and empowered to enter the I.T. space. After in-person workshops concluded, willing participants were often photographed bending their arms in the famous "Rosie" pose, while holding an Ethernet cable. We collected the pictures and compiled them for promotional purposes. See figure 6.2.

**Figure 6.2. Our mascot "I.T. Heidi" strikes an empowering pose.**
Henry Stokes

## PROJECT SUMMARY

### Budget and Method

Based on the needs identified in the 2013 I.T. Support Survey, TSLAC created a position to serve as the You Can Do I.T. program manager and to specifically serve the technology needs of small and rural libraries in Texas. In addition to providing technology-related professional development opportunities such as webinars and conference presentations, the YCDI.T. program manager develops workshop outcomes, manages logistics, and continues to develop needs-based training on technology topics for Texas library staff.

The Texas State Library and Archives Commission provides professional development to Texas library staff through the Continuing Education and Consulting (CEC) department of the Library Development and Networking (LDN) division. The CEC is funded entirely through the Library Service and Technology Act via the Institute for Museum and Library Services.

After a competitive bidding process, Carson Block Consulting was hired to develop, teach, and deliver the content. Carson's ability to be engaging, informative, and approachable when discussing technology was a huge factor in why these two-workshop series were so successful. Because so many of our small and rural libraries expressed a lack of confidence in their technology skills, communicating empowerment is at the center of this program; it was essential that the instructor and the materials were accessible without being intimidating.

Much of the program's early success is owed to Holly Gordon, the first program manager of YCDI.T. Holly spent countless hours arranging for library locations around the state to serve as inaugural workshop hosts. Holly's early dedication to this program cemented relationships on which we could build future rounds of workshop programming.

While we knew from surveys that library staff wanted technology training, the subject matter had the potential to intimidate, especially for those with limited technology skills. We hoped that using the I.T. Heidi logo and the You Can Do I.T. motto would alleviate serious technophobia. To drum up interest and reach as many people as possible, we sent out postcards with workshop information to all public libraries in Texas. We followed up with emails, newsletter blurbs, and blog posts. In areas where attendance was low, we phoned library directors and staff. Though time consuming in a large state such as Texas, personal communication helped swing the balance for those who were on the fence. In other cases, we were able to reach those that hadn't seen the workshops previously advertised. See figure 6.3.

**Figure 6.3.** Promotional postcard to promote both in-person and online YCDI.T. trainings.
Henry Stokes and Suzanne Holman

## How the Community Was Affected

Perhaps the most intriguing question addressed in the YCDI.T. classes is "Is it possible for laypeople to understand the complexities for data networks, let alone the nuances of computer hardware and software?" The short answer is a resounding "Yes!"

The longer answer—while still starting with that resounding "Yes!"—includes the learning and environmental elements that produced a mix of ingredients, creating the right atmosphere and materials to help de-mystify technical topics and make them accessible to almost anyone.

## In the Classroom/Classroom Environment

As important as the class content is (including the slides, handouts, reference resources, and quizzes), the team found that the approach to the content mattered even more. Each session began with the instructor (Carson) sharing his experiences with rural libraries and his own biases in terms of library technology and how it applies to customer service in all libraries.

Students were next asked to share a little about themselves, including either their best or worst experiences with technology. The stories (many humorous) often involved tales of triumph—or points of pain, all shared in an honest and forthright manner. The experience not only helped the class and instructor gauge the range of technology experience and attitudes toward tech, but it was also an opportunity for each perspective to be validated by the instructor and other students. The result was the creation of a "safe" environment where students felt respected and heard. This openness and directness continued throughout the day as the curriculum broached new topics. Students were encouraged to share their technology problems with answers sourced from the instructor as well as other students. No topics were off-limits, and some of the questions are among the hardest faced in libraries, including how to handle communication and personal friction issues with the technical support people the library works with.

The instructional design was heavy on experiential, hands-on learning designed to allay technology anxiety through low-stakes and high-reward interactivity. Activities were sprinkled throughout the day to help students put concepts into practice almost immediately after learning them. In all cases, the activities involved working in small groups so that everyone involved could contribute, in their own way, to working through an activity or solving a problem. The process encouraged creativity and fun among the groups.

Hands-on activities included examining data cables and other components to determine their capabilities; drawing network maps; logging in to a network router and changing configurations, disassembling desktop computers (and reassembling later), and more. For some students, this was the first time they were encouraged to explore technology in such a visceral manner, and it broke down barriers and mysteries often involved in technology subjects.

Another important aspect of the instructional design were the outcomes, or what we hoped students would be able to do after the class. We didn't expect anyone to become a computer expert or programmer as a result of the class, but we did hope that they would have a solid base of knowledge and a few more words in their vocabulary to help them communicate more effectively with the technical people in their lives.

Finally, and perhaps most important in terms of impacts, students walked out with solutions to their unique and individual challenges. Other than the pre-prepared materials, no two classes were alike, and the issues discussed reflected the unique places and people in each community.

In order to help TSLAC and the instructors gauge their own teaching effectiveness in meeting the workshop learning outcomes, attendees were asked to fill out pre- and post-surveys. A wonderful by-product of the surveys was that attendees also were able to see how far they had moved on the technology literacy continuum. A majority of attendees that entered the workshop as absolute beginners and novices responded that they concluded the day-long workshop feeling more prepared to communicate and solve technology issues at their libraries. However, maintaining this confidence post-workshop without the support of library colleagues and instructors can be difficult. In order to support workshop attendees in continuing their learning, TSLAC used their online learning platform Moodle to create and host an online version of the You Can Do I.T. workshops. The course integrates video of Carson narrating his slides and instructing in a classroom setting as well as other workshop materials such as quizzes and hands-on activities. When designing the original course materials, TSLAC and Carson worked closely to think of ways the training could be repackaged later to make the online course.

While the in-person class experience is more robust as it allows for peer learning, the online course exists as a reference for workshop attendees and those who are unable to attend the workshop in person. All of the materials, including the manuals, slides, videos, resources, and quizzes are available for free under a Creative Commons license and can be found at www.tsl.texas.gov/youcandoit.

## Success Stories

As a consultant, I'm careful to avoid recommending specific vendors, but instead focus on the ideal specifications for library systems. In the class, I recommended that even tiny libraries invest the extra money required to purchase "enterprise" grade equipment. The advantage to the library is gear that is guaranteed to perform its function for its service life (or it's replaced under warranty from the manufacturer) and it also can be configured remotely (ensuring that the library can get expert assistance from afar if they are having difficulty finding a local source). In a one-on-one conversation, one librarian pressed me hard for specific vendors for WiFi systems, and in that case I shared a few that I felt were top quality. When I saw the librarian the following year, she told me with great enthusiasm that she bought enterprise equipment and couldn't be happier with the quality and performance of her investment.

—Carson

Another librarian was having difficulties getting a strong WiFi signal in her public areas. After learning in the class about the basics of how WiFi operates (and the strengths and limitations of the various flavors of a radio-based technology), she correctly diagnosed her own problem (the WiFi antenna was located in the back of her library, causing inadequate coverage in the front). Using her new technical knowledge and vocabulary—perhaps for the first time—she was able to successfully work with her technical support person to fix the issue. She was able to describe the problems patrons were experiencing in her library, share her own diagnosis of the problem, and suggest a solution for her tech to perform. The tech agreed with her, moved the antenna, and improved connectivity for patrons.

Those are just three success stories. How many more are waiting to happen?

**Figure 6.4.**
Gwen Grimes (used with permission)

## NEXT STEPS

As technology evolves, so must our own skills, and it follows that our training for staff in small and rural libraries must do the same. Building on the success of the first two years, a third round of You Can Do I.T. workshops, entitled Teaching Technology in Public Libraries, was presented in 2017–2018. These workshops focused on building the confidence of library staff to troubleshoot their own hardware and software issues; they also received training in how adults learn best and how to create effective learning experiences for their patrons—skills library staff rarely receive in formal library science programs. As with the first two years of the program, we conducted surveys to see how You Can Do I.T. workshop attendees have been able to implement the skills they've learned in their home libraries; this information is used in an iterative manner to adapt the You Can Do I.T. program to meet our audience's needs in the future.

Lastly, we are encouraged by colleagues in other state libraries and regional consortiums who have contacted us to express interest in using these materials to teach their own workshops. If you are interested, please do reach out and let's collaborate on a way to help our library staff Do I.T.!

# 7

## Experiment, Learn, and Respond at the Salt Lake City Public Library

### Year One of the Tech League Initiative

*Tommy Hamby, Shauna Edson, Elaine Stehel*

With a full-time Nonprofit Technology Education Network (NTEN) Digital Inclusion Fellow (DIF), a budget of $10,000, and one year, the Salt Lake City Public Library set out to increase access to broadband, access to technology, and access to digital literacy education to know how to use it in a way that is meaningful and relevant to the individual. The plan was to recruit 20 volunteers, increase capacity and hours in current digital literacy education, and increase open computer lab hours in all the communities the City Library serves, but with an emphasis on areas most impacted by digital inequities.

Digital inequity can be viewed as a "wicked problem," a problem that is not fully understood until after the formulation of a solution, lacks a stopping rule, is unique, changes over time, and is never definitively solved. The solution to wicked problems can also depend on how the problem is framed, and stakeholders create different frames for the problem. Digital inequity is a social challenge that requires systemic solutions that address individual needs. Addressing digital inequities requires solutions that come from the community, rather than coming from the top down.

Like other literacies, digital literacy is nonlinear. Users are motivated to interact with technology for unique reasons, and measuring the outcomes of digital literacy education requires adopting outcomes measures that allow room for both understanding patrons' needs and allows the needs of patrons to be defined as part of the outcome evaluation process.

This chapter will explore the first year of the City Library's new digital inclusion initiative, the Tech League. During this time, the Tech League created a volunteer program, received a grant award to circulate Chromebooks and hotspots at four branches, added a second digital inclusion fellow, and refined the processes and relationship building involved in working with community partners. The chapter will end by summarizing the first year of the Tech League initiative, looking at knowledge gained from the program, and dive into projects that were learning opportunities.

## BACKGROUND

The Salt Lake City Public Library (SLCPL), established in 1898, is an eight-branch system in Salt Lake City, Utah. SLCPL is a special purpose district that is funded through Salt Lake City property taxes. It is considered a sub-component unit of the local government, which makes it autonomous from the mayor, city council, and other agencies. The statutory connection to the local government is two-fold: the mayor recommends the library's 9-member board of directors, which are approved by the city council, and the city council approves the library's annual budget. SLCPL serves a population of approximately 190,000 and is 1 of 3 public library systems in the Salt Lake Valley, Salt Lake County Library Services and the Murray Library, with which it has reciprocal borrowing privileges. Patrons from any of the systems may register their card to have access to the other systems' collections. Its mission reads, "The City Library is a dynamic civic resource that promotes free and open access to information, materials and services to all members of the community to advance knowledge, foster creativity, encourage the exchange of ideas, build community and enhance the quality of life."

## SLCPL STRATEGIC PLAN

The Library's strategic plan directly addresses the issue of access to technology. The strategic plan includes six community outcomes to guide the development of services, collections, and programs. One of the outcomes is Accessing Technology, defined as (Mission and Strategic Plan, 2017):

> Everyone in the community has access to technology and the skills to use them. Using technology is no longer optional. Without access to technology and the skills to use it, individuals may be left disconnected from friends, family, work opportunities, news, information, entertainment and much more. The City Library is already a hub of technology access, providing computers and internet access for public use. Further efforts will be made to identify those in the community without access or the needed level of skills and provide modern technologies, information and courses to keep everyone up-to-date.

SLCPL has a total of 239 public computers and free WiFi available at all locations all hours that the library is open, which includes Saturday hours at all locations and Sunday hours at 4 locations. The Main Library, in downtown Salt Lake City, has 99 computers and the Technology Center. Staff provides regular computer classes and also provides classes using a mobile computer lab at various locations within the city limits. SLCPL is one of the only locations in the city where people may use computers that offer free internet access and participate in classes to learn to use computers. In 2015 SLCPL had reached capacity with its offerings and had to turn down partnership opportunities to offer additional classes and trainings. The 2015–2016 budget request for the Technology Center included additional staff to handle the increasing workload.

## NTEN DIGITAL INCLUSION FELLOWSHIP

SLCPL was not pursuing any outside funding sources to increase capacity until it became aware of the NTEN Digital Inclusion Fellowship through its affiliation with the Salt Lake Education Foundation, which had hosted fellows in the first 2015–16 cohort. SLCPL was invited to submit an application and was accepted to be a city host for the second 2016–2017 cohort. The 2016 cohort consisted of 22 city hosts and fellows located in 11 cities across the country. For the 2016 cohort, NTEN selected libraries, literacy organizations, housing authorities, or other organizations working in digital inclusion as the city hosts.

NTEN provided funding for the fellow's salary along with a percentage for administrative costs and a $5,000 programming budget, which was matched by the Friends of The City Library, for a total of $10,000 in programming funding for the year-long fellowship. NTEN identified public libraries as one of the core mission types it would focus on in the second cohort, specifically narrowing in on adult digital literacy outcomes. NTEN's project scope guidelines use a three-tier framework to describe where each city host would be starting, in terms of digital literacy programming, and the corresponding expectations for service delivery targets at each level. SLCPL was defined as tier two, "an organization with digital literacy courses limited in geographic or time availability," and its project was to "expand digital literacy courses in size, frequency, or to other locations."

The library's senior DIF, Shauna Edson, began her fellowship in July 2016. The fellowship began with a week-long training for the national cohort and NTEN in Portland. The training covered current research on digital inclusion, best practices in community partnerships, digital literacy education, and hearing from cities that have established digital inclusion initiatives. As part of a national cohort, the fellows were able to work on digital inclusion on a micro-level while drawing support, best practices, success, and lessons learned on a national macro-level. Halfway through the fellowship, the Library had the opportunity to add a second fellow, and Elaine Stehel joined the program in January 2017. The fellows were supervised by the Adult Services coordinator, Tommy Hamby, and worked closely with the Main Library's Technology Center staff.

## THE DIGITAL INCLUSION INITIATIVE

The first steps of the fellowship were to conduct a needs assessment, define the library's digital inclusion initiative, and establish the aim of the program. The first step of the needs assessment was determining the internet connectivity level in Salt Lake City. According to the U.S. Census Bureau, 12.4 percent of households in Salt Lake City do not have internet access in the home, and an additional 11 percent of households rely on a cellular data plan with no other type of internet subscription for their connection to the internet (U.S. Census Bureau Fact Finder, 2017). According to a 2013 survey by the Pew Research Center, the key reasons people are not using the internet is 1) they do not see the need or relevancy to their life, 2) it was too difficult, 3) the cost of internet and owning a computer (Pew Research Center, 2016). To address the key reasons for low internet connectivity, the DIF planned to host a variety of digital literacy classes in the Main Library and all seven branches, establish new community partners, start a volunteer program, and research circulating devices and WiFi hotspots.

The DIF established a workgroup with the Adult Services coordinator and the Communications team to define the initiative and create a web page to function as resource for community members wanting to learn more about digital inclusion, get information on classes, and apply to be a volunteer. The initiative, The Tech League, aimed to include all community members; both those wishing to gain access to technology and digital literacy education and those wanting to donate time and resources to their communities to make Salt Lake City a more digitally equitable community. On the website, the Tech League is described as:

> The Tech League is the Library's initiative to build a more digitally inclusive community through information, workshops, events, and classes. Although many in Salt Lake City use the Internet on a daily basis, others lack access to the Internet, the devices to get connected, or the skills to use them. Without access and skills, people in our community may be left disconnected from friends and family, work opportunities, information and entertainment to improve their lives, and more. The Tech League's goal is to understand who in our commu-

nity lacks Internet access and to bring the Library's resources and tools to those individuals to foster independence, connection, and success in our digital world. (About the Tech League, 2017)

As part of the initial needs assessment and discussions with branch managers, librarians, and technology assistants, patron one-on-one tech assistance was identified as the top digital inclusion need. To address this need, the DIF established the Tech League Volunteer program. Volunteers would be placed in the computer labs to assist patrons with tech assistance, participate in outreach events, and assist library staff with facilitating classes.

The Library did not have an established volunteer program at the time, and the DIF worked with Human Resources, Communications, and the Technology Center at Main to define the volunteer program, write a call for volunteers, and develop guidelines for the volunteer program. Volunteers would only provide services that were outside of library staff job duties and/or capacity, and the Library asks volunteers to work two shifts per month for a minimum of six months. The Library asks that volunteers interested in working at the City Library wait until their six-month commitment is up before they apply for a paid position at the Library. Volunteer responsibilities were defined as:

Volunteers will facilitate digital literacy education by providing one-on-one assistance to library patrons in the Main Library Technology Center; the Creative Labs in the Main Library, Glendale Branch, and Marmalade Branch; and all Library branch locations. Volunteers will help patrons with a range of tasks including setting up an email account, password retrieval, formatting in Word and Google Docs, helping patrons navigate the Library's databases, downloading eBooks and music, and streaming movies from the Library's website. Volunteers may also help facilitate/co-facilitate digital literacy workshops and help at community events. Advanced technology skills are welcome, but not required. (About the Tech League, 2017)

Between November 2016 and June 2017, 29 volunteers donated over 920 hours assisting over 1,070 patrons at 4 of our 8 city library branch locations and outreach at community partners. While volunteer shifts are focused on assisting patrons, volunteers also benefit from interactions with patrons. The call for Tech League volunteers is open to the public, and the volunteers have a diverse range of tech skills and speak several different languages. The volunteers had unique motivations and experiences when asked about volunteering with the Tech League.

Some volunteers with careers in tech are looking to give back to their communities:

I have always been a technology guy, so I wanted to give back to the community. I have had so many opportunities in my life with technology, and when I heard about the Tech League it felt great . . . You are really changing people's lives and you are trying to build people's confidence up with technology. (Tech League Volunteer, personal communication, May 6, 2017)

Other volunteers are motivated by digital inequities and want to make a difference in their community:

I want to make sure that people have access to digital resources. What I mean by access is not just having the tools and resources but also the education. So we actually educate about what is a computer, why do I need Facebook, what is this Twitter thing? And I think we need to understand the "why" behind that and see if that is something people want to be able to use and access through their computer or using the computer at the Library. (Tech League Volunteer, personal communication, May 6, 2017)

Volunteers work to share their knowledge while gaining a sense of connection with community members:

My superpower is being a teenager. I was raised around technology, and people in their 40s and 50s haven't been around technology their whole life. I have the unfair advantage of being brought up around technology; which makes it a lot easier for me to use it. It is nice to know that I am sharing this with people that might not have had access to it or just didn't know how to use it and can take this and use it in their life and have it. (Tech League Volunteer, personal communication, May 6, 2017)

The volunteers have helped patrons sign up for email accounts; create resumes; use social media, Word, the Adobe Suite, and 3D printers; find bus routes online; download and print; do research; and log in to websites. The volunteer program enables patrons to access tech assistance that goes beyond the time and/or knowledge of library staff and offers volunteers the opportunity to contribute and connect with their community through the library.

## Community Partners

The City Library's Technology Center has been doing digital literacy education outreach for over ten years. Community partners are essential in addressing digital inequities; they provide access to community members that may not be coming into library branches due to barriers or a perceived lack of relevancy. The DIF aimed to increase digital literacy outreach to connect with more community members, and to increase awareness of the library and programs the library offers.

## Senior Centers and Income-Restricted Apartments

Beginning in January 2017, staff members and Tech League Volunteers taught weekly outreach classes for seniors 55 and older. Several of the students were from assisted or independent living facilities for low-income seniors and those with disabilities. Computer Basics classes were taught during the day on Tuesdays and Fridays, and the classes were consistently well attended by 10 to 20 seniors each week, with an average of 12 students per class. Students ranged in skill level from never having used a computer to using computers periodically with the help of family members or friends. The students were excited to have weekly opportunities to either learn new things or to practice using computers for myriad tasks to enrich their lives.

Students were also able to see how technology was relevant to their lives after taking the classes. After a four-week series of classes (Computer Basics, Basic Internet Searching, Creating an Email Account, and Creating a Facebook Account), two regular attendees came to a fifth class with their own newly purchased laptops. The students were excited to have learned enough that they were ready to start practicing on their own between lessons. The classes also helped students with learning a new language; students for whom English was not their native language were excited to have the opportunity to practice their English skills as they learned to use the computer to perform basic tasks and communicate with their family and friends.

The digital literacy education classes at the senior centers and apartments focused on the individual's interactions with technology instead of teaching "how to" use technology. Students who may have thought technology held little to no relevance in their lives learned skills to enhance their quality of life through communication with family and friends using email and social media. Students that had previously relied on family and friends to help them use technology gained autonomy to use computers without assistance and were so motivated by the classes they purchased laptops to use on their own.

## Youth Center

The Youth Center serves homeless and at-risk youth ages 15 to 24. At the center, youth have access to emergency shelter, food, counseling, legal advice, medical care, and myriad classes. Homeless and at-risk youth do not always have access to computers or broadband, and technology can help connect the youth to additional resources they may need. The library established a partnership with the center and committed to providing digital literacy classes once a week for an hour-and-a-half. We created a class schedule with practical computer classes (Word, email, social media, job searches, resumes, etc.), posted it by the front desk, and hoped some people would show up to the classes.

We just had a few participants in our classes during the first month of computer classes at the center for homeless and at-risk youth and young adults. At one point, flyers were found crushed and stuffed in a slot at the front desk. It was decided to hand them out in person. We thought about stopping the classes at the center, but we weren't ready to give up just yet. There was a way to reach out to the youth in a way that was relevant and meaningful, but we didn't know what it was.

We decided to step back from offering "classes" and set up tables with the mobile lab in a common area. We invited the youth to use the laptops for whatever they needed, and let them know that we would be happy to help with any questions they had.

At first, some of the youth would come up and take candy or chips but not use the computers. Gradually, a few of the youth starting using the computers to play games, access social media, or look up DIY projects. Some of the youth didn't appear to be comfortable sitting down to use a computer but wanted to know more about it. A participant came and stood next to his friend as he was playing a game on a laptop. His friend had to go to work, and when he left, the participant sat down at his computer. There were empty computers, but instead of sitting down at a new computer he waited for his friend to leave. Slowly, more youth started to participate.

As the youth got used to us being in the space, they started looking forward to us coming in each week. When we arrived one day, a participant was anticipating our lab and was waiting for us. He helped us set up tables, chairs, and computers.

"I am so glad you are here. I was so bored," he said. It was rainy outside and there wasn't a lot to do, but the open computer lab provided an opportunity for healthy entertainment.

We started adding topics to the lab that the youth could work on if they wanted. Katie came up with a schedule of topics that included things we noticed the youth using the computers for: cool websites, DIY projects, TED Talks, job searches, and making money online. The informal class setting started to catch on. A participant came up to us and knew what class we were teaching that day—Cool Websites—and was excited to learn.

The resource center also wanted the youth to have access to technology they may not have the chance to use often. We decided to start bringing things from the Creative Lab. Alan brought the Cricut machine, and along with Alan the youth designed and printed stickers. Matt brought the 3D printer, and everyone wanted to learn how to design and print off a ring using TinkerCad. Matt also brought a small keyboard, and he and the youth learned how to create and edit music together. By focusing on instruction through creation, we were able to shift from a teacher mode to that of a co-creator.

When the library stepped out of the role of instruction, and into the role as an active co-creator with the participants, we were able to better understand how the youth interacted with technology. After a few months of experimenting with different teaching styles and platforms, we were able to connect with the youth and provide access to technology and digital literacy education in a meaningful and relevant manner. Being reflexive in programming can make the difference between connecting with community members in a meaningful manner instead of creating programming we think or assume the community needs.

## Refugee and Immigrant Organizations

"There was this man from South Sudan, and before I started helping him he didn't really know how to use a computer, because he didn't have a computer. When I was done helping him he knew how to sign in to a computer, use Gmail, and apply for a job . . . and it warmed my heart" (Tech League Volunteer, personal communication, May 6, 2017).

The City Library invited an ESL Level 3 class from a local refugee and immigrant organization to come into the Technology Center at the Main Library. Refugees and immigrants can face transportation, time, and fear barriers to coming into libraries, as well as lack of knowledge of library services. To help address these barriers while providing digital literacy education, Shauna invited the class into the library instead of using a mobile lab to teach classes at the center.

While at the library, students signed up for library cards, toured the building, and learned how to access the events calendar to learn about programs at the branches closest to their homes. The students also learned how to use the library database and search for materials by language. Classes covered signing up for email addresses, job searching, resumes, and file management. Because most of the students did not have a computer or laptop at home, the library decided to explore teaching cloud file management using Google Drive.

Teaching cloud file management allows for device autonomy, or being able to access information from any device with an internet connection. This eliminated the need for specific software to create and read documents, as well as managing broken or lost flash drives. We found the classes worked best with small teaching segments and time to explore using Drive with assistance available.

During the first class, we signed up for Gmail addresses, learned how to find Google Drive from Gmail, and how to change the language settings to the language of the user's preference. This allowed the teacher to teach in English while students used Google Drive in the language they felt most comfortable with. The second class period focused on creating a Google Doc. The students had recently written a report on a country and wanted to format and store the report in their Google Drive. For the third class, we recorded videos of the students reading their reports in the Library's Creative Lab and uploaded them to the student's Google Drive. We also talked about attaching documents, photos, and videos to emails. The students needed to present their reports to the class, so for the fourth class we learned how to create a slideshow using Slides and how to upload images, photos, and videos to the slide deck.

The curriculum was flexible and met the needs of the students as they progressed in their ESL class. Google Drive allowed the students to communicate with friends and family around the world, and they were excited to share their videos and reports with them. Amie Rosenberg from the AAU wrote an email expressing the impact this digital literacy training has had on her students:

> This Sudanese/Eritrean/Congolese/ group arrived in the US only 3-4 months ago, had never used computers prior to their arrival and created their gmail accounts less than two months ago. This account helps to illustrate the rate at which individuals with limited English can develop the critical digital literacy skills required to access employment and most other services and benefits in the United States . . . [making films] motivated digital neophytes to persevere and practice accessing their new accounts in order to view and share their films with friends and family. (Amie Rosenberg, email to the author, February 22, 2017)

Tech League volunteers also supported the classes in the library. The volunteers assisted the instructor and were available to provide extra assistance to students. A volunteer had this to say about assisting with the program:

> There was a group from a refugee center that came in to work on their projects, they had these presentations on which countries they had all come from. Working with them gave me a chance to see how stoked they were to be here, teaching others about their culture and where they had come from, and then to interact and practice my really poor Spanish. And then see how proud they were when they were done with their finished product. (Tech League Volunteer, personal communication, May 6, 2017)

The students were motivated to learn more about technology because they were learning skills to manage their data on an easily accessible platform that allowed sharing with their family and friends. The students were in a computer lab in Salt Lake City, Utah, but through the use of technology they were sharing their work with people in Thailand, Sudan, Iran, Congo, and China. With the proper tools and education, technology can help individuals navigate geographic divides.

## Laptop Discovery Kit

The City Library wanted to create a program to help meet the digital needs of patrons that were not coming in to the library. Based on FCC Form 477 Data, we determined the lowest level of home broadband connectivity in Salt Lake City was the Rose Park, Poplar Grove, and Glendale area. Many community members using libraries in the Glendale/Rose Park/Poplar Grove community experience barriers to education. Nonnative English speakers, low-income people, and immigrants (both documented and undocumented), faced difficulties gaining employment and accessing social services, have a low percentage of internet access in the home, and experience limited access to computers/devices. Many community members in this area faced transportation, scheduling, and childcare barriers to accessing public computer labs during library operating hours.

To address this need, the library created the Laptop Discovery Kit pilot program. The Laptop Discovery Kit provided community members access to a Chromebook and hotspot service for up to three weeks and encouraged patrons to set personal digital literacy learning goals during a required orientation prior to checking out the kit. The initial year-long pilot program plan covered:

- 15 Kits including: Chromebook, Hotspot, management software, warranty on hardware, mouse, kit case, and an outline to achieve individually set goals.
- Kits may be checked out for up to three weeks. In six months, the program was assessed based on the experiences of the individuals who checked out the kit.
- To check out the kit, we offered patrons an orientation to understand the need/desire to gain digital literacy skills and set up an email account.
- Check-in: Patron was asked to complete a survey to help us understand the kit's efficacy.

Funding for the Laptop Discovery Kit came from the DIF budget and an internal Innovations Grant from the City Library. The initial pilot program had a total budget of $10,300 and covered the expenses and staff costs for 15 laptop kits to circulate at three branches. The budget included funds for: 15 Chromebooks; 15 Hotspots; 15 mice; 15 laptop sleeves; 3 wall charging stations; 15 warranties on hardware; 15 management software packages; printed promotional materials; IMS personnel, restoring device upon check-in; circulation personnel, cleaning device, checking for damage, and so on; and communication personnel for marketing and promoting the kits.

Shauna Edson created a workgroup to discuss the feasibility and plan the initial stages of the project. The workgroup included Peter Bromberg and Debbie Ehrman from the Executive Leadership Team, Tommy Hamby from Adult Services, Brian LaRue from IMS, Jennifer Briggs and Andrew Eoff from Circulation, and Gwen Page from Tech Access. Shauna also received personnel hours and a print budget from Andrew Shaw in Communications. As the DIF, Shauna worked with the group to plan and implement a sustainable timeline for the project. Shauna and Tommy trained staff at branches, Tech Access staff, and Tech League volunteers to conduct pre-checkout orientations, and worked with circulation and IMS to create circulation procedures. Shauna conducted a post-device check-in survey and compiled the data to evaluate the effectiveness of the program.

The library included security measures when designing the kits. To discourage reselling the kits, the Chromebooks and Hotspots were engraved with the library name. The Chromebooks were managed with a Google Management Software package and were set to wipe back to the image setting after every session. Both the Hotspots and the Chromebooks can be remotely disabled and are shut off three days after the due date. At that time, the kit is useless to the patrons.

The Laptop Discovery Kit pilot program measured outcomes to help determine the digital needs of the library's patrons. Library staff oriented the patrons on the kit as part of checkout procedures. During the orientation the patron set up an email account and learned the basic skills to use the devices. Patrons filled out a User Agreement and accessed a User Guide if they had further questions. At check-in, patrons completed a survey that established digital literacy knowledge gained from the project, uses of the Hotspot and Chromebook, and areas the project could improve. The data gained will be analyzed to determine if the project is reaching communities in the digital divide, determine what technology needs exist, and discover desired digital literacy education.

Prior to launching the pilot program, the program received an additional $5,000 in funding from the addition of a second DIF. The additional funding was enough to expand the program to 20 Laptop Kits, 5 each at the Main Library and 3 branches. The pilot had a soft launch in March of 2017, and within a few weeks all of the kits were checked out. Google Fiber saw an article in a local newspaper on the kits and donated $5,000—enough money to double the pilot and allow each branch to circulate 5 laptop kits. The pilot launched 4 months ago and the kit has been checked out 55 times, and there are currently 44 holds. Twenty-four surveys have been completed, and we have found 70 percent of patrons checked out the kit for both the Chromebook and Hotspot, 16 percent for the Chromebook, and 13 percent for the Hotspot. Entertainment and communication were most reported uses of the kits, followed by seeking a job, learning a new skill, and paying bills.

The future of the Laptop Discovery Kit beyond the pilot program is yet to be determined. However, the pilot thus far demonstrated the need for access to both devices and internet in the home in communities the library serves. The main expenses for the kits were covered during the initial startup phase, but the Hotspots are an ongoing expense that requires long-term funding. Cities with high circulation rates of Hotspots are often funded by grants or corporate funds. The data gathered from the pilot program will help the library determine possible funding opportunities to sustain the program.

## THE FUTURE OF THE TECH LEAGUE

During the first year of the Tech League initiative, the library was open to experimenting, learning, and responding to lessons learned and successes. Not all community partners proved to be a good fit, and several computer classes had zero attendance. It can be challenging to market to individuals who do not regularly access computers and the internet, and poster and flyer distribution played a large role in program attendance.

Top accomplishments of the first year of the program include:

- Total outputs for the 2016 Salt Lake City Public Library NTEN Digital Inclusion Fellowship

  - 12,603 training hours
  - 50 volunteers trained
  - 471 hours training for library staff

- Launching the Salt Lake City Public Library's digital inclusion initiative, the Tech League, in November of 2016

  - Slcpl.org/techleague serves as a resource for patrons and community partners to learn more about digital inclusion, digital inequities, community partners, classes, and volunteer opportunities
  - Tech League Volunteer Program: trained 50 volunteers who provided 1,000 volunteer hours and assisted 1,050 patrons

- 20 Laptop Discovery Kits: 5 each at Chapman, Day-Riverside, Glendale, and the Main Library

- ◦ As a result of the library's press release about this initiative, Google Fiber donated $5,000 to expand the program to all branches, and we will be partnering with Craft Lake City on future events
- DIFs participated in 15 digital inclusion-related outreach events, reaching 692 individuals
- Facilitated 83 in-house digital literacy classes at Main and/or branches
- Established relationships with 12 community partners to reach community members who are not coming into the library
  - ◦ Hosted 112 outreach computer classes or drop-in labs with one-on-one assistance available at community partners

The City Library will invest in and try new technologies, digital literacy classes, and programs and search out new internet adoption and device lending/low-cost opportunities. To continue its digital inclusion work, the City Library has created a Digital Inclusion Librarian position. The Digital Inclusion Librarian will work with library staff to evaluate programming, work with community partners, focus on research and development of new programming, and seek out grants and other sources of funding for new programs based on patron needs and measured outcomes.

Technology is constantly changing, and because of this, problem shaping and defining higher order concerns is an ongoing process, and risk-taking and developing new ideas is an essential part of digital inclusion programming. The Laptop Discovery Kit pilot program is an example of a risk-taking program with outcome measures that both evaluate the program and help to define the problem. Moving forward, The Tech League will build on existing digital inclusion programming and continue to experiment, learn, and respond to our patrons' technology needs and desires to help make Salt Lake City a more digitally equitable community.

## REFERENCES

Salt Lake City Public Library. "About Us: Mission and Strategic Plan." Accessed September 10, 2017. www.slcpl.org/about/mission/.

Salt Lake City Public Library. "About the Tech League." Accessed September 10, 2017. www.slcpl.org/techleague.

United States Census Bureau Fact Finder. "Presence and Types of Internet Subscriptions in Household" Accessed January 30, 2018. https://factfinder.census.gov/bkmk/table/1.0/en/ACS/16_1YR/B28002/1600000US4967000.

Pew Research Center. "13% of Americans Don't Use the Internet. Who Are They?" Accessed January 30, 2018. www.pewresearch.org/fact-tank/2016/09/07/some-americans-dont-use-the-internet-who-are-they/.

# IV

## MAKERSPACES

*Lauren Comito*

Makerspaces have captured the attention of libraries and the public alike. There is something innately disruptive to people's expectations in having a space in the library where people are getting their hands dirty, even if that is more figurative than literal. Philosophically, the idea of library as a space of creation is actually steeped in tradition. Lots of things get made in libraries but usually they are written rather than welded. There is a classic story of Ray Bradbury writing *Fahrenheit 451* on a typewriter he paid for by the hour at a UCLA library. Without a library giving him access to technology, he would not have written a classic work of fiction. Makerspaces are really cool. People are utterly fascinated by the technology in them, but putting a 3D printer into your library isn't sufficient. These chapters discuss building makerspaces around relationships and interactions with patrons. Whether it's creating mentorship opportunities or encouraging collaborations between teens, makerspaces are about more than just flashing lights and plastic widgets, they are about making communities.

As libraries start to develop makerspaces and creation labs, they tend to crop up in wealthier and more resource-rich areas. There are obvious start-up costs when libraries set up makerspaces, and as a result of this we have seen incredible makerspaces open up in affluent communities but there have been obstacles in the way of communities with fewer resources. How can you dive into buying a bunch of new tools and high-tech gear when you are still stretched thin on your book budgets and fighting every year to keep the doors open? The chapters in this section suggest that it is not a zero sum game, that assets don't need to be "pulled" from other areas to create a viable makerspace. Moreover, these libraries discovered that by investing in new resources for their patrons they developed entirely new patrons to go with it.

- Steve Teeri, an early entry into low-cost urban makerspaces, discusses the human connections and larger community-building aspect of library-based creation spaces.
- Lindsey Runyan looks at how makerspaces can be a vehicle for mentorship and collaborative learning using tools, resources, and human connections otherwise out of reach of the young adult population that she serves.
- Maria Mucino developed an organic and holistic program that included STEM and STEAM training while also addressing food scarcity, tribal history, cross-generational mentorships, and more in a library that is deeply vested in the complex community surrounding it.

# 8

## The Best Things Made in a Makerspace Aren't the Physical Ones

*Steve Teeri*

When I started a teen-focused makerspace at the Detroit Public Library (DPL) in June 2012, (www.detroitpubliclibrary.org/hype/hype-makerspace) one of the questions in my mind was, Will this be seen as a quick fad, or have staying power for the long term? The way we got started happened by, as revered twentieth-century artist Bob Ross would say, a "happy accident." Like many libraries, DPL offered teens computer classes such as How to Search on the Internet and Microsoft Office Basics. What we found was that very few teens showed interest or attended. When we spoke to the teens to find out why, they explained that they already knew all this stuff and really just wanted time after school to hang out with their friends from school and from other schools, in a relaxed atmosphere. In searching for activities that would help the teens build skills and have positive interactions, the maker movement looked like just the place to direct our time and energy. So really, the end products of making weren't even the first on our mind. At the Detroit Public Library, the question was, How can we help these kids to be their best selves with the limited time we had with them after school each weekday? Equity of access was a key consideration for us, we wanted to make sure any teen who wanted to participate would be able to. From that desire, we came to the decision there would be no cost to participate, either for attending or for materials. If we charged even one dollar for participation, it could have acted as a barrier to otherwise interested teens. I am happy to say that it worked out great, and the teens loved the programs offered, including Arduino and Raspberry Pi programming, sewing, printmaking, bike repair, and more.

Five years on, as I continue to work in the library makerspace field, interest has continued to grow, with more and more libraries taking up making and DIY activities in various forms. It's easy to focus on the tangible things that are made in a makerspace: small robots, 3D printed objects, a knitted cowl, an origami frog, a sewn denim vest for your cat. If we look deeper, the greater intrinsic value of what is taking place lies not in these artifacts that are created, but in the processes that achieve them.

## PEOPLE, NOT THINGS

A key lesson I have learned in this time is that, while the tangible things that come out of makerspaces are wonderful and a nice tribute to your work, they are not the most important things that are made therein. In fact, the tools and equipment used to make projects are also easily secondary to the most important component of the makerspace. The people. While it is easy to get wrapped up in the techno-wizardry of 3D printers and credit card–sized Raspberry Pi computers, without the right people to convey the skills, theory, and community of the tools, they really do not contain much value.

One way I like to put this is that with the right instructor, you can have a box of paper clips and a ball of yarn, and they will give you the most awe-inspiring program that leaves participants walking away enthused and amazed. One person I have worked with, Sarms Jabra, is a man originally from Ann Arbor, Michigan, and now working for the city of Detroit. Sarms started a screen-printing company called Modati while in college. He moved away to Chicago to attend law school and then returned to Michigan, taking a job with the city of Detroit to help improve its transportation system. The love of silkscreen printed shirts never left, and Sarms continues to find time to lead library workshops on the history of the technique of silk-screening. Given a few hours, Sarms can tirelessly welcome a stream of people and explain over and over what silk screen is and how it was developed, and he will assist many kids in pulling their first very own silk-screened shirt. His easy demeanor and contagious love for the activity draws everyone in and leaves them not just with a new original addition to their wardrobe, but an understanding of the reasons he loves this artistic endeavor.

Another instructor I have worked with who demonstrates how process is as important as end project is origami designer Beth Johnson. (http://bethjohnsonorigami.com/) Beth is one of a group of origami artists who are raising paper folding to the level of fine art. For their masterpieces, precise mathematical models must be created on paper. When students produce these designs, they really need to think in a creative, abstract way about the possibilities of space and position, all on a simple piece of paper. As the workshop progresses, people inevitably get stuck, and their neighbors assist in showing where a fold was missed or the correct positioning before a crease is made.

Once the intricate models are finished, you can see a sense of satisfaction in the group, that everyone arrived at the destination together, with a little help from each other, and the instructor, along the way.

Ensure you have a diverse group of instructors leading the workshops. In hiring a broad spectrum of mentors in age, gender, ethnicity, and experience, the participants will be exposed to a richer mélange of instruction.

## COMMUNITY FORMING

One of the great joys in making is seeing different people coming together and interacting—who might not have otherwise done so. At the Secret Lab in the Ann Arbor District Library (http://www.aadl.org/secretlab), many of our making programs attracted families with young kids, to groups of teens and 20-somethings, all the way up to retirees. Free equal access is one of the most compelling aspects of library making. Many makerspaces will charge either a monthly membership fee or a fee per activity. In the library maker-space niche, we can allow anyone to participate and perhaps gain interest in a new activity with others. After giving a basic tutorial in the activity at hand, people are then encouraged to work with their neighbors and ask questions of participants who have been to the program before. Weekly programs would include activities such as sewing, electronics, letterpress printing, and more. The "veteran" participants were always very forthcoming in sharing their experiences and making the new arrivals feel welcome. One interesting mani-festation of this was in our 3D printing labs. A number of late elementary school and middle school students, attending with their families, offered to help new participants, oftentimes decades older than themselves. These new participants might be surprised to see the kids so familiar with the new tech-nology and happy at their willingness to disseminate this knowledge readily. Over time, we observed new friendships develop between patrons, going so far as to exchange contact information to confirm when someone would be attending a workshop and even setting up rides to carpool together.

## STAFF OWNERSHIP

Library staff similarly benefit from makerspace being there in ways beyond having access to the equipment. It really takes a team for the makerspace to succeed, and mining skills and knowledge from staff is an essential activity. In my experience I have found that if you made a Venn diagram of library staff and DIY/maker-type people, it would be close to a perfect circle. There just seem to be a lot of crafty people who work in libraries and a lot of maker folk who really support and believe in the power and the mission of libraries.

As workshops begin to take place, other staff members may start coming up with new ideas for programs that can be offered. That is fantastic! One of the keys to keeping a makerspace going long term is new and different programming. It also helps staff to feel more invested in the space when they are allowed to assist or even run their own programs within it. One program a staff member came to me with was building a one-string cigar box guitar. I admit, I had not previously considered this as a project to offer, but loved the idea! We worked on the preparations, including building a prototype with a soldering iron. The event was very successful, with attendees leaving as newly minted luthiers. Staff at all levels should be encouraged to participate and bring their unique skills and experiences to the mix. You never know what expert crafter or maker is in your midst, but just never had a stage to be showcased.

## BUILDING CONFIDENCE

In addition to building skills, building confidence is another key outcome we should always seek. I actively encourage participants to share knowledge with their neighbors in workshops. This in turn leads to a building of confidence in the person doing the sharing, as well as the person receiving, who then sees that someone just like them has gained new skills. While staff will be on hand to field harder questions, it is always great to see the confidence built, especially in young people, who are allowed to take on some of the responsibility in resolving questions that arise. This is an intangible that is earned in the makerspace, but I really do think it is one of the most important outcomes that can be achieved. While I am happy to answer any questions posed to me, it is a great satisfaction to see a young person excitedly jump in and correctly answer the query before I've even had a chance to open my mouth to form a response. One such example of this is when people would come in to tour the HYPE Makerspace in Detroit. Questions would be posed about activities and what projects were being worked upon. One teen regular, in particular, would jump up to answer questions and act as a tour guide for the visitors. Without any prodding, his enthusiasm burst forth as he described the sewing, bike repair, and other activities that took place. By demonstration that we are all on equal footing and that anyone can volunteer to assist, it provides agency to participants to extend their role, should they desire, within the space.

## DESIGN THINKING

Frequently, attendees will want to just jump right in and make the thing that is featured. One way to slow this down and center attention on the process is to focus on the design component. Ask them to think about who this will be used by and what for. Consider offering pencils, paper, and whiteboards, if available, to sketch out ideas and compare visions with other attendees. This can be a short process at the beginning of the workshop or can even be its own stand-alone session before the actual making begins. Focus on iterations and honing an idea down to its final version. Let attendees know it's okay to make mistakes and that some of the best inventions and discoveries came from mistakes, or "happy accidents."

To get some ideas on how to teach design thinking in a learning setting, I recommend Project Zero, part of the Harvard Graduate School of Education (http://www.pz.harvard.edu/). They are producing great research into making in classroom settings and how to best frame it for participants.

## CREATIVITY, EUREKA!

Finding and harnessing the spark of creativity is one of the most elusive and important skills that anyone can achieve. While the tools can help you make your vision, the vision itself begins within the person to find what their unique idea will be. One of the best ways to promote this is to have different types of making come together to form new projects that are greater than each could accomplish individually. One example of this is having back-to-back workshops that on the face are different, but can in fact have crossover potential. If you host an Arduino electronics workshop right before a sewing workshop, you can then encourage not only the participants to stay for both, but the instructors as well. The electronics-focused people can learn how to incorporate wearables into their designs, and the clothing-focused people can learn how portable electronics can enhance the clothing envisioned. One example of this crossover in maker projects came in the form of a teen who made an article of clothing for her cat. While at the Detroit Public Library's HYPE Makerspace, we held both sewing workshops and 3D printing workshops, two common activities seen in makerspaces. This teen decided that she wanted to make a vest that her cat could wear, out of denim, and set about making the design. During this process she decided to 3D print nautical themed embellishments to realize her vision of a nattily dressed feline. With a bit of work and a few iterations, the end result was a vest that is superior to the vast majority of items in my own wardrobe. While the vest was exquisite, and a great object to take home, it was the process of envisioning, designing, and realizing the garment that was the true achievement.

## FORMING MINDSET

Altruism can be baked right into the making as a key component. When planning making workshops, consider the idea of giving away the end results as a part of the activity. This can come in the form of knitting or sewing clothes that are then donated, to custom holiday cards to be distributed at a senior center. If the item is made to be given away from the outset, it encourages a focus on the process of creating and finding a reward in the quality of the thing, and the reward of giving as opposed to possessing. I've found giving to be quite contagious, and as people see that it will be going to a thankful recipient, people get excited and want to add their contribution to the donation. Gift projects around the holidays are also a great idea to promote giving. It may also save the attendee who had previously forgotten to make a special gift for that special someone. You have helped to save (insert holiday here)! Strive to make inclusion over exclusion as a goal. Ensure that everyone feels welcome and able to participate however they are coming to the activity.

## PARTING WORDS

When selecting the tools that will be in your makerspace, and the things that will be made with them, give more consideration to the people who will be teaching and using these tools. Seek out experienced teachers from a wide spectrum of backgrounds and viewpoints. While the destination of making something is an excellent goal, the journey of getting to that point truly is even more important than the end product.

This creative problem solving in makerspaces is profound and extends well beyond the projects in the makerspace. When looking at what will be made in your makerspace, it is important to look at the equipment and materials that will be housed and made available, and most important of all—the people. Keep in mind that just as the best things in life are free (they really are!), the best things made in a makerspace aren't the physical ones.

# 9

## Library Makerspaces and Interest-Based Learning as Tools for Digital Equity

*Lyndsey Runyan*

All young people should be able to reap the benefits of living in a more connected world with digital access to learning, connecting, and creating. In order to be prepared for future education and career opportunities, teens must have a mastery of digital skills. Unfortunately, from scarcity of access to internet-connected digital devices and limited internet connectivity to limited informal digital education opportunities due to systemic inequities of class, race, and other kinds of systemic privilege, many youth in low-income neighborhoods do not have access to meaningful digital instruction, tools, and mentors to guide them in an increasingly digital world. While adults tend to assume that all teens have smartphone access, the Pew Research Center's Teens, Social Media, and Technology report says that 12 percent of teens have no cell phone access and 30 percent of teens only have a basic cell phone (Lenhart, 2015). And in addition, according to the Opportunity for All report from the Families and Media Project (Rideout and Katz, 2016), many low-income families are under-connected. Most learning, including digital learning, takes place outside of formalized education environments. In fact, only 5 percent of an average American's life is spent in classrooms (Falk, Dierking, 2010: 488). Public libraries can introduce teen patrons to an even bigger digital world, not only by providing access to technology (which by itself cannot level the playing field for those affected by digital inequity) but also by offering guidance, mentorship, and interest-based digital programs.

In April 2015, Multnomah County Library (MCL) opened its first dedicated creative technology space, Rockwood Makerspace, in a branch library located in the Rockwood neighborhood straddling Portland, Oregon, and the neighboring suburb, Gresham. The overarching goal of the makerspace is to create a collaborative learning environment that will contribute to mitigating

Rockwood neighborhood's widening digital divide by providing opportunities for hands-on informal learning and offering the neighborhood access and mentoring in new and exciting technology. It does not work to simply provide those who experience digital inequity and lack of privilege with the tools to connect them to the digital world; but rather, libraries must also provide community spaces, relationships with mentors, and interest-based programming to encourage digital participation and twenty-first century skills. Multnomah County Library hopes to address these project goals in our space: increase teen confidence; build knowledge and skills in digital media and making; encourage youth to be leaders in the makerspace; and ensure 40 percent of participants are young women or gender non-binary identified.

## COMMUNITY NEED

Multnomah County Library's mission is to empower the Portland Metro and adjacent communities to engage in lifelong learning by offering diverse opportunities for all patrons to learn, read, build community, and create. In addition to being the oldest public library west of the Mississippi, Multnomah County Library is Oregon's largest public library, serving 757,371 residents of Multnomah County, about one-fifth of Oregon's population. Multnomah County has the greatest number and largest proportion of people of color of any of Oregon's 35 counties. The population is roughly 72 percent white (alone, not Hispanic or Latino); 11 percent Hispanic or Latino (of any race); 7 percent Asian; 6 percent black; 2 percent American Indian/Alaska Native; with 4 percent reporting another race, or two or more races (American Community Survey, 2014). To address the needs of a community in which 20 percent of residents speak a language other than English at home and 15 percent of residents are born outside the United States, Multnomah County Library has significantly expanded its services to speakers of languages other than English, including hiring library staff who speak the languages represented in different neighborhood libraries. See figure 9.1.

The library was deliberate in its choice of Rockwood Library for its first makerspace, as it is one of Multnomah County Library's smallest branches at only 6,435 square feet and also one of the busiest of its size with about 136,299 patron visits from July 2015 to June 2016. Rockwood Library was originally built in 1963 in an effort by the Library Association of Portland, predecessor organization to Multnomah County Library, to expand library service to an underserved part of Multnomah County between two existing library branches. (Multnomah County Library) At the time, Rockwood was said to serve about 20,000 patrons annually. In 2014, that number was

**Figure 9.1.  Multnomah County Library's Rockwood Branch**
Lyndsey Runyan

around 82,491. (American Community Survey, 2014). The library was renovated in 1999 and now serves an expanding multilingual and multicultural neighborhood.

The history of Rockwood is one of a recently incorporated neighborhood that has long been ignored by the municipalities around it. The area was agricultural farmland for many years, primarily growing strawberries (Lesowski, 1985). Before the City of Gresham, neighboring city to Portland, was forced to annex Rockwood in 1987 due to sewer issues, Rockwood was unincorporated Multnomah County. Rockwood began urbanizing in the 1970s with the construction of large apartment complexes and a new Boeing manufacturing plant in Gresham, attracting more diverse residents (Moore and Fenn, 2010: 9). Throughout its recent history, Rockwood has faced boundary confusion due to rapidly changing city borders during the 1980s. During this time, the City of Gresham annexed many parcels of land outside of its borders in unincorporated Multnomah County. Many suburban Gresham residents expressed resentment at having to include Rockwood in their city long after annexation. A 2012 article in the Gresham *Outlook* quoted one resident as saying, "The neighborhood has just gone so downhill. I know that we here in Gresham do not like being linked to Rockwood as part of Gresham. It has a bad rep and will take years to change if that is possible. We would like to be linked to a more neighborly, less crime-ridden area. And that isn't Rockwood." (Stine, 2012) For many years, Rockwood was known by the pejorative nickname "Rockhood." (Hébert, 2013: 3) Rockwood's reputation continues to be a "bad" neighborhood or one unknown by inner-Portland residents.

Adding to the confusion about boundaries since annexation, many Rockwood residents have a Portland mailing address, due to being served by the nearest post office, located in the city of Portland. Due to this mailing address discrepancy, Rockwood, Gresham, and Portland residents are confused about what city Rockwood belongs to (Stine, 2012). Rockwood only started getting municipal attention starting in 1998 with the first of several Gresham city plans for development, the Central Rockwood Plan, which sought to incorporate light rail transit and mixed use development. Since then, there have been various development plans and even a federal program operating from 2002 to 2007 called "Weed and Seed" whose purpose was to weed out undesirable elements of the neighborhood and invest in community organizations (Moore and Fenn, 2010: 9). In 2002, residents of Gresham voted to designate Rockwood as an Urban Renewal Area. It took until 2015, due to ballooning costs and a poor economy, to form a feasible plan with a completion timeline for an actual Rockwood Town Center, only a few blocks east of the library. Rockwood Rising, the current name for this project, is expected to be a cultural and geographical center for Rockwood featuring retail space, locally owned restaurants, a marketplace, a technology center, and business incubator with the goal of being opened in 2018. In short, Rockwood is finally getting the attention and investment it needs as a vibrant, growing, and diverse neighborhood in East Multnomah County. Many worry that these measures may have the unintended consequences of displacing low-income residents through gentrification, a problem plaguing the Portland Metro region.

Young people in Rockwood face language, opportunity, and digital divides that limit their education and career success. They do not have the same systemic privileges as their counterparts in other neighborhoods in the Portland metro area. Thirty-four percent of Rockwood's population is under 18 years of age, and 75 percent over the age of five speak a language other than English at home. The City of Gresham, in their Rockwood Rising presentation, reports that there are over 70 languages spoken by Rockwood residents (Fuhrer, 2016: 2). Rockwood has the lowest median income of any neighborhood in Multnomah County and the highest rate of residents living in poverty at 28 percent (American Community Survey, 2014). Ninety-five percent of the students at the nearest elementary school make use of the free or reduced lunch program. Reynolds High School, the nearest high school to the library, had the lowest graduation rate of any school in Multnomah County with only 67 percent of students graduating in 2016 (Oregon Live, 2016).

Rockwood Library is an important resource in a neighborhood where there have historically been very limited physical spaces for community to gather, learn, and create together. While in other neighborhoods, community members would have access to community centers, parks, coffee shops, and even their own homes for community space and internet access, many Rockwood residents use the bustling community library as their primary source of computer and internet access. From July 2015 to June 2016, Rockwood patrons logged 43,000 sessions on the library's public computers and Chromebook laptops, compared to much lower numbers at other comparably sized library branches. Rockwood has a large and committed volunteer base of local patrons who help with programs like homework help, summer reading, and other administrative tasks at the library. From July 2015 to June 2016, Rockwood volunteers contributed about 4,188 volunteer hours, surpassing many of the library's larger branches. Multnomah County Library was excited to locate the first creative learning space in this well-used and well-loved library, in an effort to expand library services to include interest-based learning for teens and as a way to address geographical digital inequity in Multnomah County. The library located the makerspace in Rockwood to give an economically struggling and underprivileged community access to digital and maker tools, classes, and collaborative space to inspire digital skill building. There was a decision to focus on teens during this project in recognition of an inequity of out-of-school learning opportunities for Rockwood's underserved youth population. Another contributing factor to locate this project at Rockwood was the library's desire to engage the high number of teens at Rockwood Library expressing interest in having more activities, programs, and services for teens.

## BUDGET, RESOURCES, METHODS, AND PROCESS

In 2014, Multnomah County Library applied for and was awarded a three-year, $300,404 Community Technology Grant from Mt. Hood Cable Regulatory Commission (MHCRC) to build a 1,065-square-foot addition to the Rockwood Library to serve as a teen makerspace. For about 20 years, MHCRC's Community Technology Grants have offered funding throughout Multnomah County to nonprofits, educators, libraries, and local governments to support use of community technology resources for a public benefit. This grant was amplified by The Library Foundation, an organization

**Table 9.1. Project Budget**

| Cost Category | Grant Funds | Foundation Funds | Library Funds | Partner In-Kind | Total |
|---|---|---|---|---|---|
| Personnel | $40,144 | $0 | $475,550 | $0 | **$515,694** |
| Education | $0 | $37,500 | $0 | $9,615 | **$47,115** |
| Equipment and Supplies | $64,960 | $47,762 | $47,762 | $0 | **$112,722** |
| Infrastructure Construction | $3,300 | $1,550 | $1,546 | $0 | **$6,396** |
| Facilities Construction | $192,000 | $310,550 | $296,377 | $0 | **$798,927** |
| Fees | $0 | $0 | $25,914 | $0 | **$25,914** |
| Miscellaneous | $0 | $0 | $33,565 | $0 | **$33,565** |
| Overhead | $0 | $0 | $17,898 | $0 | **$0** |
| Total | **$300,404** | **$397,362** | **$898,612** | **$9,615** | **$1,540,333** |
| Percentage of Total | 19.5% | 25.8% | 58.34% | 0.62% | 100% |

Lindsey Runyan

committed to private fundraising for Multnomah County Library. MCL paid the bulk of the costs associated with this project, taking on an extra $300,000 in construction costs due to unforeseen regulatory costs. The total project budget was $1,562,231. See table 9.1.

The most valuable and expensive resource for the makerspace is the staff who work extremely hard to make the space successful. In fact, there are even more staff working on this project than are reflected in the project budget; they contribute to committee work, direct public service, mentorship of teens, volunteer coordination, community outreach, training, and more. Rockwood Library staff work very hard to build relationships with teens, adapt to be co-learners of new technology alongside learners, and support Rockwood youth through mentorship. "It is the staff, not the stuff!" is often used to describe how important relationships are to the success of teen makerspaces. When this project started, there was only one dedicated staff member, a project coordinator who led staff teams, built community relationships, and set up the infrastructure for the space to function. The plan was for direct programming to be done by existing librarians and library assistants at the branch. The library did not account for how busy bilingual branch staff already was with their regular duties. Adding significantly more duties dedicated to the makerspace proved overwhelming for many branch staff. After initial makerspace programming began in April 2015 in a small meeting room at the branch, the project coordinator recognized the need for a dedicated staff member for this project. After advocating for this staff need, in October 2015, the library added a 30-hour temporary makerspace staff member. These hours were reallocated from other unfilled library positions. In 2016 a permanent 40-hour a week position was approved in the library's budget. Later that year, the library added another 20-hour temporary position that became permanent the following year. As of this writing, the makerspace has two dedicated staff contributing 60 hours a week to the makerspace, branch staff working 15 hours a week in the space, and a full-time coordinator supporting the makerspace and similar project expansions to other branches in the library. All staff work to build community in the makerspace, instruct on basic digital skills, and co-learn more advanced skills alongside youth.

The makerspace is not only supported by staff but also by community volunteers, both adults and teens. Forty volunteers have contributed 1,600 hours in the makerspace from the makerspace grand opening in April 2016 to April 2017. Volunteers contribute to the makerspace community weekly by mentoring teens, either as peers or adults with digital interest. In the first two years of the makerspace, 18 adult volunteers have acted as mentors, guides, instructors, and role models in the makerspace. Most have volunteered at the makerspace since the new addition opened in April 2016. Library staff trains new adult volunteers every three to six months. Adult volunteers are trained in mentoring teens, connected learning theory, techniques for building community, teaching, planning and reflecting, giving encouragement, growth mindset, and more. They often work one-on-one with teens, helping to support whatever ideas teens want to explore in the makerspace. Engaging community members as volunteers in the space fulfills one of the most important goals: to provide role models working in science, technology, engineering, and math fields to teens. One of Rockwood's longest-serving volunteers was recently spotlighted in a Multnomah County Library volunteer services newsletter:

When not at Rockwood, Seph works as a computer programmer and builder of puzzles for escape rooms. He describes himself as part of the Maker community, hobbyists in the Ben Franklin mold who experiment with science and technology. Despite his own significant experience, Seph admits to having learned by teaching the students and experimenting with Rockwood's equipment. He believes the most effective way to encourage kids is to start a project himself; soon someone is looking over his shoulder wanting to know how to do that. And that, according to Seph, is his mission: showing them possibilities and hoping they take it from there. (Childs, 2016)

Adult volunteers have been important in supporting makerspace youth in creation and exploration of their interests and skills and risk taking and failure management. Volunteer mentors help create a supportive and collaborative learning environment where they help youth overcome challenges.

There have been 22 teen volunteers over the course of the makerspace project, who act as peer mentors to fellow teens during the daily drop-in programming. Rockwood is lucky to have such a large and committed group of teen volunteers, mostly as a result of great connections between long-time staff and the community. The makerspace was able to draw on this pool of teens to build up the group of teen volunteers. The library initially convened a group of willing teen volunteers to act as a sounding board for the building design, initial programming, equipment, and tool ideas. From this group, 12 volunteers were recruited to start in the new space. From 2016 to 2017, this group has grown to engage over 20 teens, who are provided with support and training on how to be library teen leaders, peer mentors to other teens, and part of a collaborative learning environment. Through several local youth employment nonprofits, the makerspace has been lucky enough to hire three teen volunteers as paid summer interns. This teen leadership pathway is vital for the success of the program, allowing teens to direct program goals and feel ownership of the makerspace.

Multnomah County Library was fortunate to have a generous grant and funding from The Library Foundation to acquire cutting-edge equipment for the makerspace. The equipment focus was on tools that were well reviewed and recommended by other libraries, makerspaces around the country, and local partners and instructors. While it is clear that "it is the staff, not the stuff" that makes the space successful, there is no denying that innovative equipment and tools are a significant attraction for the space and that building confidence, skills, and knowledge using the makerspace equipment is a large part of makerspace outcomes and goals. The library bought equipment and software on the topics and skills of instruction in the makerspace, which include 3D Design, Art and Design, Electronics, Engineering, Sewing, Video/Audio, and Game Making/Coding. See table 9.2.

**Table 9.2. Rockwood Makerspace Equipment**

| Name | Make/Model | Purpose |
|---|---|---|
| Windows Laptops | Lenovo Y40-80 | Gaming, Design, Game-Making |
| Mac Laptops | MacBook Pro | Design, Art, Video/Audio, Game Making |
| iPad Tablets | iPad Air 2 | Video/Audio, Robotics, Art, Gaming |
| Small 3D Printer | Lulzbot Mini | 3D Printing |
| Large 3D Printer | Ultimaker 2+ | 3D Printing |
| Laser Cutter | Epilog Mini 18 | Design, Art |
| Vinyl Cutter | Silhouette Cameo | Design, Art |
| Desktop CNC Mill | OtherMill | Design, Art, Electronics |
| Sewing Machines | Singer 4411 Heavy Duty | Sewing, Engineering |
| 3D Scanner | Structure Scanner | 3D Design and Printing |
| Digital Scanner | Epson Perfection | Art, Design |
| Wide Format Printer | Epson Artisan 1430 | Art, Design, |
| Solder Stations | Weller WLC100 | Electronics |

Multnomah County Library had previous experience planning interest-based digital media learning programs for teens before working on the makerspace project. In 2012 the library partnered with local science museum Oregon Museum of Science and Industry (OMSI) on a joint Institute for Museum and Library Services (IMLS) and MacArthur Foundation planning grant to engage teens in "mentor-led, interest-based, youth-centered, collaborative learning using digital and traditional media." The goal was to create a teen learning lab prototype for other libraries and museums in the county wanting to start similar services and programs. The library used the learning, best practices, and the framework from the collaboration with OMSI, as well as best practices from teen council youth leadership, in designing the Rockwood makerspace several years later. Teen councils are a youth-driven advisory group at many public libraries that help steer youth programming, collections, and improved library services for teens. For many years, teen councils at MCL branches have helped guide and even lead teen programming at the library. Rockwood Library's teen leaders met with architects to give feedback on the building design, helped guide the makerspace program selection, and drafted patron safety agreements using an equity lens process in collaboration with staff and county attorneys.

Through the IMLS/MacArthur grant, project staff were connected with the YOUmedia Learning Labs network, a national community of practice of over 30 sites like the makerspace around the country that support each other's work, share and create resources together, problem solve, and develop what learning labs in libraries and museums can do to further institutional missions. Being supported by other sites via this community of practice, both online and in-person, is an invaluable resource for creating and sustaining this project. Library staff are able to use lessons learned by colleagues around the country and tweak them to fit particular communities. The network was also an amazing sounding board for sharing and finding ideas, questions, and issues that came up while both planning and implementing this project.

## Methods/Process

To address inequity and lack of interest in formalized education experienced by many youth, advocates and researchers support broadened access to connected learning—learning experiences that are interest-driven and peer-supported and that lead toward educational, economic, or political opportunity. Connected learning takes advantage of the opportunities provided by new kinds of digital technology to more easily link home, school, community, and peer learning environments; support peer and community connections based on shared interests; and create more learning pathways for underserved youth. Connected learning focuses on deploying digital media equitably to reach and enable those who otherwise lack access to learning opportunities, in particular, youth that do not have access to class, race, or other kinds of systemic privilege. In the Connected Libraries Surveying the Current Landscape and Charting a Path to the Future report, a publication from an IMLS-funded team of faculty and researchers at University of Washington and University of Maryland, libraries are some of the best space to provide connected learning spaces, "Modern libraries represent ideal environments for supporting connected learning. They are centers for knowledge creation and sharing, they support self-directed and interest-based learning, and they are inclusive public spaces that bring many different groups together" (Hoffman et al., 2016: 11). To bridge the digital divide and to encourage connected learning, the Rockwood makerspace focuses on providing Rockwood teens with adult and peer mentorship; space, equipment, materials, and organizational support for hands-on and digital classes, camps, and open project time; and a consistent schedule of classes and open lab time for youth to explore interests, passions, and collaborations. Along with connected learning, the makerspace uses the theory of HOMAGO, a term invented by a team of MIT researchers led by Mimi Ito to describe the increasingly engaged learning modes of how teens interact with new digital media. The theory of HOMAGO—hanging out, messing around, and geeking out—has grown to encompass all kinds of informal learning experiences. HOMAGO is based on the learning theory of constructivism, which posits that the most impactful learning occurs when participants have hands-on experiences coupled with planning and reflection rather than the traditional transfer of knowledge from teachers to students (Ito, 2010). All of these learning theories focus on the experience of the learner rather than the subject or skills being taught. See figure 9.2.

The Rockwood makerspace offers three different kinds of programming based on HOMAGO and connected learning theory: daily drop-in labs, structured workshops, and week-long camps. The intention is to offer all three tiered levels of learning for youth to be able to engage in digital media, activities, and community in the makerspace. The makerspace is open after school four days per week and Saturday mornings, offering drop-in Open Labs, where youth can self-direct and explore projects and activities they are interested in with the support of makerspace staff and volunteers. Informal instruction is focused on project-based learning during Open Labs, providing introductory projects for designated topics and makerspace equipment. When youth first come into the makerspace, staff welcomes them, shows them around the makerspace, and does a mini-interview asking youth about their interests. Teens get started by working with staff, volunteers, or other teens on a beginning project to learn about the equipment or topic. Examples

**Figure 9.2.   Rockwood Makerspace**
Lyndsey Runyan

of projects include: 3D printed word necklaces and keychains, laser cut book-marks and stencils, CNC milled dog tags and stamps, machine cut vinyl stick-ers and greeting cards, stop motion pixilation and claymation, coding obstacle courses for robots, and audio beat making and recording looped beatboxing. Open Lab is the most popular makerspace program with youth dropping in to learn digital skills that relate to other spheres of their lives: for example, replicating their own artwork on wood using the laser cutter, making birth-day cards using the craft cutter, sewing a pillow using the sewing machines, taking apart broken electronics, and more. One of the key ways the maker-space has connected youth interest is by encouraging youth to create and manufacture gifts for their friends and family. In fact, connecting learning inside the makerspace to teens' experiences outside the space and providing digital instruction provided at the point of need is a large part of what allows this particular program to thrive. Some Rockwood teens, who live in nearby homeless shelters, report that Open Lab is their favorite library program because of the freedom to choose their own activity. Because most of these young people's lives are structured with very limited ability to choose even what they will eat for meals, choice is extremely important.

Open Lab is supported by two staff members, one to two volunteer adult mentors, and one to three teen mentors. This program can serve up to 18 youth at a time and in summer often has a waiting list. The daily consistency of Open Labs occurring most days after school and during school breaks is another reason it is successful; participants do not need to remember what day the makerspace is open. Teens know if they show up after school or when school is out, staff and volunteers will support them in creating whatever they can imagine.

The makerspace also offers more structured workshops, where either staff or contract instructors teach youth a specific skill or topic. In the last year, the makerspace has offered workshops on many topics, suggested by makerspace teens, including: video game design, animation, costuming, eTextiles (sewing with electronic elements), fashion, coding, robotics, 3D and 2D design, stop motion, laser cutting, beat making, and more. Makerspace workshops are an opportunity for youth to get more in-depth introduction and instruction on a new skill or topic than during Open Lab but without much risk or a lengthy time commitment. Often workshops are focused on instructing youth on digital skills necessary to complete a project. Most workshops involve basic instruction on software or apps to create or work on vector graphics, graphic design, animation, film editing, audio creation and editing, coding, programming, game design, 3D design, and more. Most youth have little to no experience working with these kinds of digital tools before makerspace workshops and need time to understand and practice using them. Typically there is an instruction sheet, where instructors or staff have created step-by-step instructions with screenshots so that youth can replicate workshop projects later and learn at their own pace. Makerspace culture embraces mistakes and failures as well as iterating on methods that do not work. Due to that kind of shift in expectations from school, youth express that they are more willing to try new digital skills and work collaboratively to solve problems.

Lastly the makerspace provides camps, in-depth program series that allow teens to dive in deep to a topic or skill. Often these interest-based and digital production-centered camps take a topic first covered in a one-off workshop and expand on the learning. For example, the beginning video game design workshops were easily expanded into a camp where youth worked together to create a video game using MIT's game design software, Scratch. Two youth took their interest and skills developed during the camp to finish a game and entered it into a regional game-making contest, the Mythos Challenge. These youth actually were among the winners, earning further opportunities to collaborate with professional video game developers on their game. One of the most popular camps was in response to youth requests for a camp to build their own skateboards. The makerspace partnered with a local skateboard group and shop, S.M.A.R.T. Collective, to offer a five-day camp that combined digital design using Adobe Photoshop and Illustrator to design stencils and stickers for both their boards and helmets, engineering skills to put the boards together, and skateboard riding skills when makerspace staff and mentors took youth out to learn to skateboard. Other makerspace camp topics include: digital photography and editing, film making, do-it-yourself gift making, Minecraft world building, screenprinting, eTextiles, and more. Connecting youth interest to camp topics makes digital learning more relevant to teens, provides in-depth time to really learn skills, and also connects teens to experts, careers, and educational opportunities outside the makerspace.

Due to community requests, the makerspace collaborates with teachers and nonprofit organizations to provide customized workshops for groups of teens. While this was not part of the original plan for makerspace programming, it is an important way to connect and make inroads with the local community, particularly with Rockwood teens who wouldn't find the makerspace on their own. Staff is able to demonstrate through hands-on, relevant, and fun workshops that the makerspace has something to offer all teens who are interested in learning more digital skills. Past partners have included Girl Scout troops, alternative schools, charter schools, public school teachers, nonprofit organizations that serve LGBTQ youth, immigrant youth, youth of color, girls, robotics clubs, and others.

While currently the makerspace has a great recipe of programming that fits the community needs, it did not start out this way. Staff tried different topics, workshop lengths, number of sessions, and days and times. Some were wildly successful, like the skateboard building camp, and some were not even attended by one participant, like the camp offered on building catapults and trebuchets. The main lesson learned about makerspace programming is to really listen hard to what the community and teens in the space want to learn and find ways to connect with expert instructors in those topics, to offer lots of time to explore and drop in, and to offer camps during school breaks when youth have more time to commit to learning outside of school.

## COMMUNITY IMPACT

In its first year, 2016, the makerspace offered 298 teen programs, serving 688 youth who checked into the makerspace 2,060 times. The makerspace is primarily serving youth from the neighborhood; 83 percent of participants came from a five-mile radius around Rockwood Library. The makerspace served 39.7 percent young women and gender non-binary individuals, just under the goal of 40 percent. Fifty percent of the racial/ethnic identities represented in the makerspace were from underrepresented communities in science, technology, engineering, and math careers and education (National Action Council for Minorities in Engineering, 2017).

By investing in the makerspace, MCL is able to help bridge Rockwood's digital, economic, and language divides and systemic inequity by providing a collaborative learning space, innovative equipment, materials, instruction, mentors, and leadership opportunities for teens. Youth that do not have many systemic privileges will still have access to innovative technology and wraparound support for learning. Outcomes measured are that youth will improve their knowledge, interest, and confidence in STEAM after attending a makerspace program. Staff members conduct makerspace evaluation every six months for a two-week period, with teens filling out surveys answering questions related to the outcomes. In 2016 staff evaluated 79 youth during two weeks during both May and December. Evaluation of the makerspace in 2016 found that:

- 71 percent of participants improved their understanding of a science, technology, engineering, arts, or math topic after attending a makerspace program
- 66 percent of participants improved their confidence in digital tools, software, and equipment after attending a makerspace program
- 55 percent of participants stated that they have more interest in a science, technology, engineering, arts, or math topic after attending a makerspace program
- Many of the remaining 45 percent of youth surveyed already reported having high interest in STEAM before coming to the makerspace, which remained after participating

In addition, youth reported that at the makerspace program they attended:

- 85 percent said they felt welcome and comfortable
- 75 percent said they learned something new
- 65 percent said they had the chance to make something cool
- 50 percent said they worked with another teen on a project
- 47.5 percent said they felt part of the community
- 17.5 percent said they taught someone else something

Even more important than gaining technical skills and knowledge of a digital topic, makerspaces and connected learning environments help youth develop soft skills or "people skills" needed to be successful in all careers and educational pursuits. While difficult to assess, makerspace staff report youth displaying many soft skills, also known as twenty-first century skills, outlined by the Museums, Libraries, and 21st Century Skills report. Youth engage in problem solving, critical thinking, thinking creatively (both individually and with others), viewing failure as opportunity to learn, collaborating with others, and more (2009).

As this was the first implementation project of its kind at Multnomah County Library, the library learned many lessons about what went well, what could be improved, and how to measure success. The library is committed to improve on our lessons learned for any future creative learning spaces and digital inclusion projects at MCL including sustained engagement by the intended audience, dedicated staffing and training to prepare current staff for changes, and meeting patrons at their level of digital comfort while nudging them to try new challenges.

While both the community and youth were asked what they wanted from the makerspace, there was not a sustained plan to continue gathering feedback from the community. It is best practice that when creating a new service or program for youth, that youth co-create, help guide the project, and keep staff accountable for incorporating teen interest (Braun et al., 2014). While staff did gather youth input from Rockwood Library teen volunteers, for the next creative learning project, the library intends to convene a group of advisers that includes the intended audience before and after launching in order to get feedback and guidance.

Fortunately, Multnomah County Library had the resources to create several new positions to be dedicated to the makerspace. Before embarking on this type of project, it is important to evaluate staff capacity for the amount of training, enthusiasm, and flexibility the new service will require. It is also important that MCL was flexible in the approach to staffing and training in the makerspace. The library needed to take staff and volunteer turnover into account and develop onboarding strategies for new staff in order for the program to be successful. In the future it would be best practice to train staff from multiple branch locations as well so that training is spread out among the entire library system. While sometimes challenging due to schedule constraints, direct service staff should be involved in the planning of new services and programs like the makerspace as they work the most closely with the community and have valuable insights on how to engage the neighborhood.

The makerspace is clearly having a positive and measurable impact on Rockwood youths' digital literacy, science, technology, engineering, and math proficiency by providing opportunities for interest-based digital and maker learning so that youth develop the skills to succeed in future education and find sustainable careers. It should not be assumed that, because more of today's youth than ever before have access to digital tools, they are becoming digitally literate on their own. It should also not be assumed that libraries need huge budgets, expert instructors, or even expensive equipment to provide equitable interest-based digital media programming to inspire communities to become digitally connected. A key factor to address digital inequity that worked for Multnomah County Library's makerspace included being deliberate about locating the new digital learning program in a neighborhood that is traditionally and currently underserved and is overwhelmingly populated with lower income patrons who do not have class, race, and other identity privileges. In addition, finding engaged staff and volunteers that are willing to co-learn and mentor, structuring learning as project-based and hands-on, and providing consistent programming made the project successful, inspiring youth to become creators of digital media instead of only passive consumers. In an increasingly digital world, library patrons need their libraries to offer opportunities to learn how to be digitally literate and even contribute to the digital landscape by engaging in interest-based learning and creation.

## REFERENCES

American Community Survey. "2014 ACS 1-year Supplemental Estimates." *American Factfinder.* Accessed May 19, 2017. https://factfinder.census.gov/faces/nav/jsf/pages/searchresults.xhtml?refresh=t#none.

Braun, Linda W., Maureen L. Hartman, Sandra Hughes-Hassell, and Kafi Kumasi. "The Future of Library Services for and with Teens: A Call to Action." Young Adult Library Services. 2014. Accessed June 27, 2017. www.ala.org/yaforum/sites/ala.org.yaforum/files/content/YALSA_nationalforum_final.pdf.

Childs, Donna. "Maker Mentor." Multnomah County Library Volunteer Spotlight. 2016. Accessed June 16, 2017. https://multcolib.org/blog/20161026/volunteer-spotlight-seph-bain.

Falk, J. H., and L. D. Dierking. "The 95% Solution: School Is Not Where Most Americans Learn Most of Their Science." *American Scientist,* 98, 486–493. 2010.

Fuhrer, Josh. "ROCKWOOD RISING: A Development Project by the Gresham Redevelopment Commission." Gresham Redevelopment Commission. 2016. Accessed June 3, 2017. https://static1.squarespace.com/static/562927b9e4b0ddf1eefce333/t/57b25a3746c3c465f610d9ce/1471306314049/Rockwood+Rising+Presentation-for+GRDCAC+6-8-16.pdf.

Hébert, Alison. "Beyond 'Rockhood'—Stigma, Diversity, and Renewal in a Suburban Portland Neighborhood." Portland State University honors thesis. 2013. http://pdxscholar.library.pdx.edu/cgi/viewcontent.cgi?article=1020&context=honorstheses.

Hoffman, K. M., M. Subramaniam, S. Kawas, L. Scaff, and K. Davis. "Connected Libraries: Surveying the Current Landscape and Charting a Path to the Future." College Park, MD; Seattle, WA: The ConnectedLib Project. 2016.

IMLS Office of Strategic Partnerships. "Museums, Libraries, and 21st Century Skills." Institute for Museum and Library Services. 2009. Accessed June 27, 2017. www.imls.gov/assets/1/AssetManager/21stCenturySkills.pdf.

Ito, Mizuko. *Hanging Out, Messing Around, and Geeking Out: Kids Living and Learning with New Media*. Cambridge: MIT Press. 2010.

Lenhart, Amanda. "Teen, Social Media and Technology Overview 2015." Pew Research Center. April 2015. www.pewinternet.org/files/2015/04/PI_TeensandTech _Update2015_0409151.pdf.

Lesowski, Lynda. "Rockwood, Wilkes Typify Diversity of East County," *Oregonian* (11/3/1985). *The Historical Oregonian* (1861–1987).

Mikkelsen, June. "Rockwood Library History." Multnomah County Library. Accessed May 14, 2017. https://multcolib.org/rockwood-library-history.

Moore, Stephanie, and Dr. John B. Fenn III. "Rockwood Cultural Asset Mapping Winter 2010 Building Community and Engaging Residents." Sustainable Cities Initiative. Eugene: University of Oregon. 2010. Accessed June 7, 2017. https:// scholarsbank.uoregon.edu/xmlui/bitstream/handle/1794/10582/RockwoodAsset Map_ReportOpt.pdf;sequence=1.

National Action Council for Minorities in Engineering. "Underrepresented Minorities in STEM." Accessed June 27, 2017. www.nacme.org/underrepresented-minorities

Oregon Live. "2016 Oregon High School Graduation Rates." 2016. Accessed May 29, 2017. http://schools.oregonlive.com/grads/.

Rideout, V. J., and V. S. Katz. "Opportunity for All? Technology and Learning in Lower-Income Families. A Report of the Families and Media Project." New York: The Joan Ganz Cooney Center at Sesame Workshop. 2016. http://digitalequityfor learning.org/wp-content/uploads/2015/12/jgcc_opportunityforall.pdf.

Stine, Mara. 2012. "Border Dispute." *The Outlook*. January 23. Accessed June 3, 2017. http://pamplinmedia.com/go/42-news/18701-border-dispute.

US Census Bureau, Population Division. "Annual Estimates of the Resident Population: April 1, 2010 to July 1, 2013." Accessed May 29, 2017. https://factfinder .census.gov/faces/tableservices/jsf/pages/productview.xhtml?src=bkmk.

# 10

## Improving Education with Library STEM Programs and Access to New Technologies

*Maria Mucino*

In this chapter, we provide a glance of how equal access to technology, library partnerships, and STEM (Science, Technology, Engineering, and Math) library programming can make a community thrive. Based on the absence of parental involvement in Guadalupe children's lives, we placed an emphasis on the mentor-apprentice program for this community. While the mentor teaches new technologies, they also provide encouragement and nurture aspirations as research has shown that when libraries, schools, families, and organizations work together to support learning, children are more likely to succeed (Henderson and Mapp, 2012).

The Guadalupe Branch Library, part of Maricopa County Library District, is located in Guadalupe, Arizona. The community is home to a combination of 6,000 Native American Pascua Yaqui Tribal members and Latino residents. The median household income in Guadalupe is $36,649 (US Census Bureau, 2010), which is far below the median household income in Arizona and the United States, $50,225 (US Census Bureau, 2015), and $55,777 (US Census Bureau, 2016) respectively, and nearly one in three people are living below the poverty line. According to the Department of Education (2015), three out of every five 4-year-olds in the entire country do not attend early childhood literacy programs, and in Guadalupe it is four out of every five; these preschoolers are already behind their wealthier peers by the time they start school. The lack of access to formal education in Guadalupe, Arizona, for 0–5-year-olds may be the result of a combination of multiple barriers, mainly language and economic hurdles. Often, these children have never been enrolled in a school until they reach kindergarten. For the next age group, the 2010 census indicates that in Guadalupe, Arizona, 25 percent of the population are children between 5 and 17 years old and within the same poverty level, one out of three live below poverty. The only school in Guadalupe is Frank Elementary School, part of the Tempe School District and a Title I school. Kids in middle and high school attend the Tempe and Kyrene school district options, outside the Town of Guadalupe. These numbers may look disheartening, but rather than dwelling on the problems of the community, the library took action. After an environmental scan and community assessment in 2014, the library began strategically implementing outcome-based library programming. This not only helped to improve the children's education, but also helped children to succeed in this new information-based and highly technological society, where everyone needs to develop their capabilities in STEM to a much higher level than in the past.

## DIGITAL EQUITY

Since learning and job opportunities have mostly gone digital, Guadalupe students require access to technology to complete their homework; residents require access to technology to apply for a job, to get a food handler's card, or to check their children's school grades, and so on. Thus, digital equity is one of today's essential necessities.

For the past five years, Guadalupe Library has focused on using technology to transform learning experiences with the goal of providing greater equity and accessibility. However, technology access and equity are a difficult issue that embraces other complex elements, like socioeconomic status, racial and ethnic identification, place, language barriers, ability, among many others. In an effort to bridge that gap, the library provides to its customers computers with high-speed broadband and loans a variety of tablets with free WiFi access to low-income families in the community. However, the real challenge is making sure the customers are aware of those services and that they have the skills to use the technology. With innovative library programming and an assortment of technology gadgets, library staff are working to ensure access to high-quality technology and content, individualized for the entire Guadalupe community.

## LIBRARY PROGRAMMING

In order to offer impactful library programming to a large range of children, the library divided the youth into four categories, 0–4-, 5–7-, 8–12-, and 13–17-year-olds. This allowed staff to create purposeful library programming targeted toward each group with three elements in mind; edutainment (education and entertainment), STEM, and food insecurity.

For the 0–4-year-old group, we created two programs. The first program transformed the traditional Storytime into *Story-Brunch*. It used the same elements of *Every Child Ready to Read*, but added some STEAM concepts and built-in use of iPads where parents and children follow along reading the books while learning how to scroll, swipe, and drag on the iPad. The staff also added a craft using food where kids were able to savor and discover vegetables and fruits for the first time. Food for this program was provided through a library partnership with Harvest for Humanity Foundation, a nonprofit organization with the mission to "strengthen community by using and educating local volunteers to growing fresh quality produce to provide for those in need."

The second program was geared toward 3- and 4-year-olds. It consisted of a series of ten structured sessions about colors, sizes, numbers, shapes, and STEAM, where children and parents together listen to stories, play rhyming games, match letters, explore print and its message, and actively construct their learning using a SMART Table to develop a collaborative work and foster positive social engagement among parents and children while utilizing new media. The time of the program was intentionally scheduled to tie in closely to lunch time and by the end of the activities, children received a free lunch sponsored by Kids Café St. Mary's Food Bank, a library partner helping with hunger in the community. For this particular program staff distributed the Project Outcome Early Childhood Literacy Survey from the Public Library Association (PLA) to participants in order to measure the impact of services designed to improve early literacy and learning skills to prepare children to succeed in school as well as to aid the library in analyzing the data and sharing results with partners.

For the second group, 5–7-year-olds, the greatest need was reading. According to the Arizona Department of Education (2015), there were approximately 84,500 students enrolled in the third grade in 2013 in Arizona. In reviewing the scores on the reading portion of the 2013 Arizona Instrument to Measure Standards (AIMS) test, 17,440 students were in the "approach" category and 3,000 students were in the "falls-far-below" category. The latter number did not take into account students that meet the requirements for exemption status such as: English Language learners with less than two years of instruction in English and students with an Individualized Education Program (IEP) for reading and/or language. The same year at the local elementary school in Guadalupe, 66 percent of third graders failed the reading portion of the AIMS test (Arizona Department of Education, 2013). Simultaneously,

Arizona passed the *Move on When Reading* legislation, which was designed to promote early identification and intervention for struggling readers so that students are reading at grade-level by or before the end of third grade. Thus, the library implemented *Read to Succeed!* a program geared to improve the academic achievement of at-risk first grade students. The goal of the program was that all children would show measurable academic growth by improving their oral language and early literacy skills through the use of direct instruction and digital media, such as e-books on iPads, to make reading appealing to children. The core components of the program are Reading A–Z, an online database of e-books and lesson plans, and Raz-Kids, the online component for children's instructional and independent reading levels. First grade teachers from the local school referred children to the library program after their first DIBELS (Dynamic Indicators of Basic Early Literacy Skills) testing. Tutoring groups, with the help of local college students through a partnership with Arizona State University, include two to four children reading at the same level; reading sessions include an iPad station, writing station, and literary station. The second DIBELS testing at school determined the continuity of the children in the program. This has resulted in bridging the technology and literacy gap at the same time.

The library developed a series of programming for 8–12-year-olds because they are the largest group as far as population, such as STEM Up, GEMS (Girls in Engineering Math & Science) and Make It! These programs started in 2013 in close collaboration with third to fifth grade teachers from Frank Elementary School. The goal was to ensure that library staff develop library programming that relates with the science curriculum for those grades. For instance, if the science theme of the week was physics: solids, liquids and gases, the library would offer a project-based activity such as *Make it! Soaps and Fizzy Bath Bombs.* Not only was the program fun, but children were able to take home and use their own products while providing them with an opportunity to continue learning outside the classroom with creativity, excitement, and innovation in science learning. For these tinkering programs participants were divided into groups to make their own creations and used iPads to research concepts. Occasionally groups did not have the results they wanted, however, the program was designed to allow children to have more than one iteration without feeling frustration or disappointment. This has been one of the best collaborations and partnerships the library has ever developed. After a full year of library STEM programming, the percentage of passing science scores for students in fourth grade increased from 29 percent in 2013 to 36 percent in 2014.

The 13–17-year-old group constitutes almost 17 percent of Guadalupe's population and needed special attention. According to the Department of

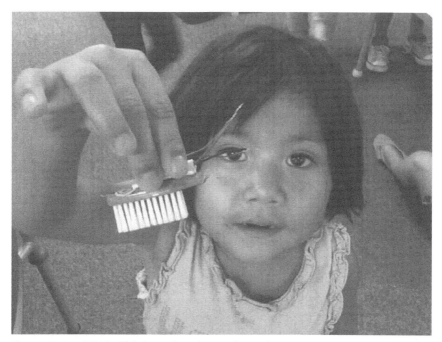

**Figure 10.1.   GEMS (Girls in Engineering Math & Science)**

Education, the high school dropout rate decreased from 10.9 percent in 2000 to 5.9 percent in 2015 nationwide, while Arizona and Guadalupe reported 6.7 percent and 18.7 percent dropout rates, respectively. The Library created the Digital Audio, Video, and Photography Club, Teen Court Club, and Young Innovators Club as after-school library programming to engage this group and worked diligently to put together a mentor-apprentice program to empower youth in the community to help change negative and delinquent behavior in their peers, to foster civic and technological engagement, and to model the value of education.

## MENTOR-APPRENTICE PROGRAM

The first after-school library program created within this apprenticeship model was the Digital Audio, Video, and Photography Club. J. Peter Mortimer, a long-time contributor and former picture editor of *Arizona Highways Magazine* and photojournalism professor at Arizona State University was the first mentor. He spent four hours per week during a six-month period teaching Guadalupe teens about digital photography, frames, color, setting, and the use of the equipment. After a few indoor sessions, he took the teens out into the community to capture their everyday lives. The following sessions included shooting, reviewing pictures, and getting feedback from Mr. Mortimer. He then recruited professional colleagues to mentor alongside him and to continue the program after his first six months. Teens were able to check out cameras for the day and have computers available to download their work. The interest in some teens grew at an incredible pace; the library created a quarterly museum-like exhibition of their artwork. A local program, *Su Vida* from COX Communications, ran a two-minute inspirational story of one of the teens. "She was only going to go as far as High School, but once her photography was noticed, she changed her mind and direction, and now she wants to go to college" (*Su Vida*, 2016). Following the digital photography program, Guadalupe teens have been introduced to audio, podcasting, film recording, stop motion animation, and green screen equipment. The Pascua Yaqui Tribe is known for its rich oral tradition. Instead of using a written language to document their history, these indigenous people simply relied on their verbal language to share their history, customs, rituals, and legends through vivid narrative. However, when the elders pass away, their stories, myths, and legends go with them. Pascua Yaqui teens are using the library equipment to record their grandparents' anecdotes and some of them hope to keep their history alive. This club has revived a long-standing oral history project spearheaded by Pascua Yaqui Tribe in Tucson, Arizona.

The Teen Court Club was the second after-school library program purposely developed to help Guadalupe teens learn about the law, develop leadership and technology skills, network with professionals, and perform tasks beyond what they may have initially felt capable of. This program is a three-way partnership with Guadalupe Municipal Court, Maricopa County Superior Court–Juvenile Court Division, and the library. Judge Lilia Alvarez has been the mentor since its inception in 2015. Judge Alvarez is the personification of the American Dream. The daughter of farm workers with a passion for treating people with fairness, respect, and dignity, she has been able to inspire many Guadalupe teens to continue their path to college. With the library resources and her network of professional colleagues, teens had the opportunity to learn how to include technology in their everyday lives. This club has demonstrated its success in a number of ways. First, a solid core group of approximately twenty teens regularly attended the weekly meetings to learn about the law, the government, and new technologies. The participants have facilitated and adjudicated over fifty court cases diverted from Juvenile Court. Participation in the Teen Club has brought opportunities for employment and internships through Arizona@Work. This is a program sponsored by the Maricopa County Human Services Department that provides employment, skill development, computer classes, and educational support via the Workforce Investment and Opportunities Act. Fourteen teens were able to take advantage of this opportunity in the first year and almost half of them worked at the library helping during the summer lunch program *Read & Feed* sponsored by St. Mary's Food Bank in partnership with Arizona Department of Education and USDA's Summer Food Service Program.

In October of 2016, five teens received scholarships to visit Washington, DC, to kick off the first Annual Guadalupe Teen Court Ambassadors Program. Four out of the five teens had never been on a plane, taken the subway, or gone away from home. From checking their itinerary online to figuring out their food budget, those teens finally saw computers as a tool and not as a gaming device. The same year in November, one of the participants was honored as second-place winner in the essay competition at the AZ Teen Court Summit. Throughout the program, teens have learned how to use many computer applications and programs that helped them create their own website to showcase their accomplishments. Out of the first cohort of teens, three of them are in college pursuing law, political science, and conservation degrees, one is going to college this fall, three are juniors, and the rest are still in the ninth and tenth grades. Guadalupe Teen Court Club members are trained to serve in the roles of peer jurors, lawyers, bailiffs, clerks, and judges in adjudicating cases of juveniles who have committed an offense eligible for diversion. Technology and library electronic recourses have been made available for them as tools to accomplish their jobs. This program was the recipient of the 2016 Achievement Award from the National Association of Counties for being the only Teen Court in the entire state of Arizona that is held in a library setting with a judge as their leader.

The *Young Innovators Club* is the third after-school program designed for this age group with mentors and advisers. The library recognized that access to new technologies connects teens to all kinds of information and gives them opportunities to be creative and solve problems. For the low-income and disadvantaged teens, access to this program has the power to change their social structure by allowing them to become empowered and engaged. The program offers access to 3D design and printing, coding, robotics, electronic and STEM kits. The main goal of the program is to create an environment where teens realize they can learn to do anything they want despite their circumstances. These activities exemplify the core principles of STEM programming while tinkering and making. Martinez and Stager (2013: 32) refer to making as the "active role construction plays in learning" while tinkering is a mindset—a playful way to approach and solve programs through direct experience, experimentation, and discovery.

The club generally meets once a week and the library provides technology, tools, electronic and print resources, consumables, and a place to meet and work. Sessions are structured using the peer-coaching and apprenticeship model; these techniques build collaboration, act as a problem-solving medium, and reduce isolation among participants. Although one of the main intentions for this program was to promote innovation while learning new technologies in an apprentice workshop style, establishing that concept was a complex task. The long-standing history of discrimination against Latinos and Native Americans in Arizona has resulted in a distrust of organizations. In addition to economic and social hurdles such as transportation, language and cultural differences may have prevented community participation. Thus, in order to effectively engage this group, the library focused on building empathy for how culture influences the community and by recognizing culture-specific factors that impact participation in order to schedule programming. The library also put emphasis on developing the ability to see and genuinely understand the culture to connect and build trust with the youth.

Initially, the library sought out assistance to mentor Guadalupe teens from the local Intel® employee volunteer program, the closest microprocessor manufacturing facility to the library, to bring expertise and enthusiasm to the program. In 2015, staff from HeatSync Labs (http://www.heatsynlabs.org), a local grassroots nonprofit makerspace—they called themselves a *hackerspace*—began to assist as mentors within the Guadalupe community. Partnering with both organizations allowed library staff to concentrate on finding resources, such as local grants, as well as identifying youth in the town interested in innovation and entrepreneurship and providing them with a place to meet and share their interests while growing cohesively in the community.

## FUNDING

At the beginning, resources for these programs were entirely grant-funded, a little over $18,000 by means of two Library Services and Technology Act (LSTA) grants and four STEM mini-grants from Maker Media, Inc., Arizona Center for Afterschool Excellence, BirdBrain Technologies, and the Arizona State Library, Archives and Public Records. After one full year of programming, the library presented a proposal to the administration to create seven new Maker/STEM kits that can travel to all seventeen branches, granted that the programs and equipment would first be used at Guadalupe to allow staff to create samples and guidelines for the rest of the library system staff. The latter initiative continued, allowing the library to introduce newer technologies to teens in Guadalupe.

## EQUIPMENT

Deciding what tools, kits, and consumables to acquire took a careful analysis of the space, staff, and community. After all, the budget was limited, and needs were abundant. We relied on the first edition of the *Makerspace Playbook 2013* school edition, library colleagues, and the library assessment to complete the task. The first acquisition was a Printrbot kit to be assembled at the library as part of a program; this turned out to be the inspiration for one of the teens to 3D design and 3D print jewelry and gifts for teachers and friends. Another teen 3D designed and printed a refrigerator handle to replace a broken one at home. Unlike many libraries, teens are welcome to 3D print anything without paying for the service as long as it is their original design. Downloads from Thingiverse or other similar sites are not allowed. Creativity and purpose are the two main components of free 3D printing. The library also procured an XYZprinting da Vinci, a very sturdy and economical 3D printer; iPads; a SMART Table 442i collaborative learning center; a sewing machine; a couple of soldering irons; LEGO Mindstorms; 10 Makey Makeys; 4 graphic calculators; 17 Playaway Launchpads; a variety of robotic kits, such as littleBits, Arduino, Ozobots, Spheros; VR equipment; STEM kits, like Snap circuits, Vortex, Osmo; small tools; and consumables such as wire, solder, LEDs, batteries, motors, buzzers, and more.

## PARTNERSHIPS

When the Guadalupe Library joined forces with local government and organizations, the community wins. However, not all of the partnerships were successful. The take on partnerships is that if the relationship tilts to one side, it's not a beneficial partnership anymore. Sometimes the library needed to leave on good terms or stopped the service or program and found another organization for which a partnership could be more mutually beneficial. Throughout this process the library learned that the most successful partnerships were differentiated by the ability to accomplish four basic tasks: 1) clearly define the purpose of the relationship, 2) understand that the whole of the partnership adds more than the sum of the individual parts, 3) develop collaborative work process by sharing resources and expertise, and 4) create a sustained momentum by keeping everyone apprised of failures and/or successes, minor and vast, while focusing on the long-term goal of community change. In celebrating small successes, the library once celebrated one of the 32 children in the Read to Succeed! Program. After 10 weeks this child was able to move from at-risk level to tutoring level, while in a different community and circumstances, three out of five kids would have shown the same improvement.

Realistically, it would have been impossible to offer 836 library programs with a total of 26,897 attendees in three years in a small semi-rural library with 4-FTE (6 staff members total). Without the collaboration and participation of at least eight core organizations and individuals, including the town officials, the library would not be able to claim that STEM library programs and new technologies improve education. State test scores have increased and the high school dropout rate in the town has declined, but the most noteworthy change within the community has been the building of trust. The library is now a voting member of the Town's Education Committee and Youth Programs and the Pascua Yaqui Tribe's Guadalupe Prevention Partnership Network.

The driving principle behind the *Mentor-Apprentice Library Program Model* is that over time the library fosters community collaboration and moves beyond community engagement. We have learned that building relationships with members of the community and fostering collaborations with its trusted leaders and organizations motivates participation in library programs. We also recognize the importance of careful selection of outside partnerships and collaborators, the ones that are willing to understand the community and their beliefs and are genuinely involved in the progress of the community.

Staffing the library was also challenging at one point, so having a diverse and bilingual staff in both Spanish and Yaqui, or Hiaki, languages was critical to gaining trust and facilitating the programs. Hiring staff within the community is ideal, as they are the best advocate for the library efforts, they serve as a bridge to the community, and they are a role model for the youth.

Although Guadalupe is a small semi-rural library, it has the great advantage of being part of a large library system and without the support of administration, this type of programming would not have been possible. In fact, needs assessment and environmental scans are now the baseline for developing library programming in all branches within the district.

The collateral success with purposely based library programming has fluctuated to about an 8–10 percent increase in circulation and foot traffic. On a typical afternoon at the library, you will find high school students borrowing a graphic calculator or an iPad to do homework, a group of children playing–learning fractions using the SMART® Table, first graders borrowing Playaway Launchpads, a teen designing a Minecraft character to 3D print, a group of teens with their tech mentor building a cardboard pinball machine with LEDs, a Makey Makey and a computer attached to it for game scoring, a group of school-age kids requesting to play-code with Spheros, and another group of teens sewing their own costumes with conductive thread and LEDs to get ready for Halloween or Phoenix Comicon. Except for staff and mentors, adults or parents are seldom at the library. This presents a challenge in itself, so common behavior manners are in place for everyone, including mentors and staff, such as: 1) say please, 2) say thank you, 3) apologize if you make a mistake, 4) smile and have a great attitude, 5) share, 6) clean up after you finish, and 7) praise others for a good action. Library staff focus on positive reinforcement and are encouraged to read or listen to Dr. Fay's Love and Logic philosophy.

With STEM library programming and access to new technologies, the library is helping bridge the literacy and technology gap and slowly becoming the town's community hub for connected learning. We recognize there is still a lot to be done. However, the first bricks of the foundation are set for learning to thrive in the Town of Guadalupe.

## REFERENCES

Arizona Department of Education. Arizona report cards, accessed April 18, 2017. www.azreportcards.org/.

Arizona Department of Education. Statistics, research and reports, accessed July 9, 2017. www.ade.az.gov/menus/eleven.asp.

COX. *Su Vida.* Selena Larios, accessed June 15, 2017. www.cox7.com/video/selena -larios/.

Henderson, A. T., and K. L. Mapp (2002). *A New Wave of Evidence: The Impact of School, Family, and Community Connections on Student Achievement.* National Center for Family and Community Connections with Schools. Austin, TX.

Martinez, S. L., and G. Stager. (2013). *Invent to Learn: Making, Tinkering, and Engineering in the Classroom.* Torrance, CA. Constructing Modern Knowledge Press.

US Census Bureau, Guadalupe, Arizona Population: Census 2010 and 2000 interactive map, demographics, statistics, quick facts, accessed May 27, 2017. http://censusviewer.com/city/AZ/Guadalupe.

US Census Bureau, Median Household Income in the United States: 2015, accessed May 26, 2017. www.census.gov/library/visualizations/2016/comm/cb16-158_me dian_hh_income_map.html.

US Census Bureau, Quick Facts Arizona, accessed May 26, 2017. www.census.gov/library/visualizations/2016/comm/cb16-158_median_hh_income_map.html.

US Department of Education. National Center for Education Statistics. Status Dropout Rates, accessed June 8, 2017. nces.ed.gov/programs/coe/indicator_coj.asp.

US Department of Education. New reports show greater need for access to high-quality preschool for American children, April 2015, accessed March 21, 2017. www.cen sus.gov/library/visualizations/2016/comm/cb16-158_median_hh_income_map.html.

# V

# TECHNOLOGY FOR EMPLOYMENT AND BUSINESS

*Lauren Comito*

Job search help has become one of the primary ways libraries assist patrons with technology use. Any public librarian in service for more than six months will have formatted, printed, and quite possibly edited scores of resumes in addition to assisting with filling out online forms and facilitating Skype interviews. Once again we find ourselves at a technological step up in how we serve our public. Yes, librarians will always have to assist with resumes, but what if they moved to helping patrons become their own boss? Technology is hugely important in employment and in business development. At the same time it is complicated and challenging to access if there are language or digital literacy barriers. How can libraries effectively make technology a tool for community members to be economically empowered?

The chapters in this section look at technology as an essential tool of business. There is information here about technology training as part of refugee and new immigrant services wherein new arrivals are given tools to help them flourish in American culture in their own language, allowing them to access basic computer applications needed for employment and self-empowerment. The same library (incredibly) is also fostering entrepreneurial skills like complex problem solving and innovation along with tech training. Finally, while libraries are giving answers, sometimes the questions change right out from under us.

- The team at St. Paul Public Library broke out of the walls of the library and the bounds of monolinguistic training to bring technology to immigrants and refugees in Amharic, Hmong, Somali, Spanish, Tigrinya, and Karen to make deep connections with technology and the library in new populations in their community.

- Another group at St. Paul Library created a workforce innovation center serving entrepreneurs, creative professionals, and teens that goes beyond simple job search efforts and includes innovation as a tool of career and community development.
- Multnomah Library created a complex and informative technology skills survey to better assess and respond to the genuine (and sometimes surprising) needs of their community with a particular focus on problem solving skills and creative solutions to complex issues.

# 11

# Evolution of Community Services in Saint Paul

## Rebecca Ryan and Pang Yang

In 2010, the demand for help with job search was outstripping available community resources at Saint Paul Public Library(SPPL), workforce centers, and community-based organizations; low levels of digital literacy prevented too many Saint Paul residents from applying for entry level jobs and participating in Adult Basic Education and Work Readiness Certification programs; and new immigrants who are non-English speakers faced multiple barriers to building workforce skills and getting and keeping jobs. At the time, Saint Paul had a population of 285,468, the second largest city in Minnesota. The Saint Paul Public Library has thirteen buildings and a Bookmobile, and it is the only city-run library system in the Twin Cities metro area. The overarching challenge the library sought to address was the gap in broadband access and literacy along lines of income, race, and ethnicity. The library also set out to explicitly provide services to communities isolated by poverty, race, and immigration status, as many in these communities were not being invited in to library buildings and not equitably accessing free library resources and instruction.

The Federal Communications Commission (FCC) published Broadband Adoption in Low-Income Communities in March 2010, a report that examined this phenomenon across the United States. Its conclusions, particularly that "broadband access is a prerequisite of social and economic inclusion (and low-income communities know it)," and "libraries and other community organizations fill the gap between low home broadband adoption and high demand," both reflected and influenced SPPL's work in this area (Dailey et al, 2010).

During the recession years, 2008–2010, SPPL saw an increased community need for computer skills and job-search training. Meanwhile, the

demographics of Saint Paul, like the rest of Minnesota, had changed rapidly—particularly post-2000. The library had been receiving, on average,
about 700 requests per week with regard to digital literacy, job search, and
resume building. In 2009–2010 these requests had increased 34 percent over
the previous year. Library buildings consistently reached capacity for these
services. In 2010, it was difficult to ascertain precisely what portion of Saint
Paul's population had meaningful internet access, although it was estimated
to be about 75 percent. Within communities of color, particularly immigrant
and refugee communities, the number of people with reliable broadband
internet access, workable devices, and enough digital literacy to take advantage of the opportunities afforded by the digital realm was much lower. The
percentage of people accessing library services from immigrant and refugee
communities in particular was also lower,

Saint Paul's population had changed quickly, and that change was expected to be reflected in the 2010 census numbers. In 2011, however,
concrete demographic information was difficult to come by as census data
had not been released. Once the data was released, certain difficulties were
revealed. Saint Paul has large communities of people hidden inside data
markers. For example, US-born African American populations have much
different needs than Somali or Ethiopian-born populations, yet all groups fall
under the generic heading of "black." Additionally, Saint Paul has a large
Hmong and Hmong-American community, as well as, at the time, a growing
number of Karen refugees from Myanmar. Despite their differences, both of
these communities fall under the "Asian" heading and also obscure the results
of other, smaller populations within the city, such as those with Vietnamese
or Cambodian heritage.

There is still a need today to disaggregate data on city maps. "African"
languages encompass Somali, Oromo, and Amharic, not to mention others
in smaller numbers, but it remains difficult to pinpoint these communities on
the map. See figure 11.1.

These data shortcomings matter, because in 2010, SPPL received a
$300,000 grant from the John S. and James L. Knight Foundation to teach
computer classes and job search skills outside the library in languages other
than English. SPPL used the term "Work*place*" as the brand for its jobs, career, and small business resources and support. The Knight grant was written
to accomplish two goals: to make the Work*place* mobile since demand for
service within library buildings was near capacity and to provide multilingual
services throughout the community. This project presented an opportunity to
extend learning and economic opportunities to communities in Saint Paul for
whom English is a secondary language. The goal of SPPL was, in collaboration with private and public partners, to meet the high demand for job search

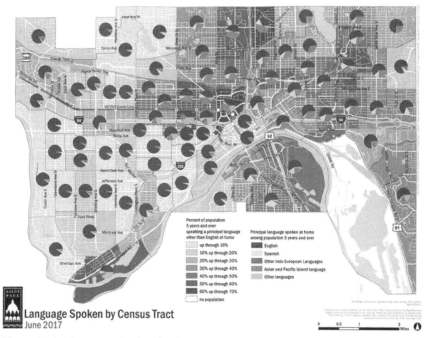

**Figure 11.1. Language Spoken by Census Tract, June 2017**
St. Paul Department of Planning and Economic Development

and technology skill training by extending this service outside library facilities, to communities not traditionally seen in high numbers in library buildings. Its secondary goal was to test the feasibility and efficacy of providing library services outside of library buildings.

Setting up the mobile workplace required hiring the project manager; procuring hardware, software, and a vehicle to serve as the mobile lab; hiring and training three cultural community liaisons; partnering with community-based organizations; and delivering WORK*place* classes in multiple languages. The library assumed at the beginning of the project that Spanish, Hmong, and Somali would be the languages in highest demand and that formal classes would be held in the same locations over the next three years. See figure 11.2.

The grant budget allocated most funds toward personnel. Once the project manager was hired, she began researching several program elements: languages/ethnicities and relevant locations for classes, relevant partner organizations, equipment, supplies, and logistics. At the time there were very few similar programs in the United States. The programs that delivered mobile digital literacy primarily relied on a bookmobile-like setup that was beyond SPPL's budget. In reality, once the project manager began contacting

**Figure 11.2.  Mobile Lab**

organizations, it became clear that there were many underutilized computer labs throughout the community. To reach the people most in need and most disconnected from public services, a mobile lab was still necessary. It was initially planned to lease a vehicle through the City of Saint Paul's Public Works Department to transport the mobile equipment. Only city employees are allowed to drive these vehicles, and the liaisons, who would be teaching the classes, were contracted employees with The Friends of the Saint Paul Public Library. The most cost-effective solution was the purchase of a vehicle by The Friends. This led to its own series of questions, ranging from where to park the vehicle to how to transport and store laptops. The resources of the public library and ingenuity of its staff members played a role: the library had a garage space available in an old building, and the community and digital services manager had military experience. She suggested Pelican cases, since this is what the military used to transport technology. This way, unlike the bookmobile, which was restricted in what sites it could visit due to the need for a large parking space, the mobile lab was only restricted by whether or not a location was wheelchair accessible, since the Pelican cases had wheels and could be transported relatively easily.

The project manager was also tasked with producing a job description for the liaisons and setting up a structure with The Friends of the Saint Paul Public Library. Seventy-six applications for the three part-time cultural liaison positions were received (that, in itself, a comment on the lack of available jobs at the time). The candidates hired had exceptional skills and experience working with and within their communities and, in some cases, had previous experience teaching technological and WORK*place* skills in languages other than English. A few of the liaisons were not as familiar with Saint Paul communities and partner organizations, requiring significant assistance from the project manager in identifying locations, partnering, and publicizing opportunities. Initially, the project manager cast a wide net to find people and organizations to talk to. Given the aforementioned lack of exact geographical knowledge relating to particular cultural communities, the bookmobile librarian proved an extremely helpful resource. In some ways, the mobile lab and the bookmobile were mirror images of library services outside the traditional building. Bookmobile stops generally serve locations with a concentrated, underserved population, farther away from library buildings, whether that meant schools without libraries, public housing developments, or senior high-rises. In several instances the bookmobile librarian shared his extensive knowledge of Saint Paul's racial and ethnic geography based on his experiences delivering mobile services. Other helpful organizations included the Saint Paul Community Literacy Consortium, a consortium of adult basic education providers including the school district and community-based organizations, and Saint Paul's district councils and resident-planning organizations.

The Mobile WORK*place* began offering classes in June of 2010, starting with 10 classes each week. In discussions with partner organizations, feedback identified further community needs. As a result, two additional classes were offered, with translation into Karen, Amharic, and Tigrinya. An initial surprise was that, out of the organizations approached, not a single one turned down the opportunity to partner with the library. As the project continued, the project manager could better ascertain which partners actually had an audience for the service versus those who just wanted to try it out. These initial classes were offered both in existing computer labs and with the mobile lab.

When the mobile WORK*place* began offering classes, the wireless modem and router that provide the mobile WORK*place* with internet service functioned well in some locations but not in others. An additional service plan and antenna were purchased for the router, and the firmware was updated. These additions allowed the mobile WORK*place* to provide the most reliable mobile internet connection for all users at classes. As the project years continued, mobile internet service improved by leaps and bounds and also became cheaper.

In the first year of operations, several assumptions made by the library were disproved. First, classes continued to be offered in locations with computer labs and not solely through the mobile lab. Through Broadband Technology Opportunities Program (BTOP) funding, many Saint Paul nonprofits had added computer labs to their organizations. They quickly discovered what it actually entails to program and run a successful computer lab, and many were unable to fully use the equipment they already had. In some instances there was no good instructor, in others no curriculum, and in still others the lab was allowed to fall into disrepair and was not regularly maintained or scheduled. These all became opportunities for the mobile workplace to partner with that organization and fulfill organizational and community needs and project goals. For example, one organization that traditionally focused on Spanish speakers had an increasing number of Somali clients, so the mobile workplace taught a computer class in Somali at Comunidades Latinas Unidas en Servicio. Another example found an existing computer lab totally booked for ELL classes while the job search students had no access—once again, enter the mobile lab and a teacher who spoke Karen.

Secondly, the variety of language needs was much wider than those most reported and most used—Spanish, Hmong, and Somali. Partners quickly identified digital literacy training needs in Karen, Amharic, Tigrinya, Oromo, and English. In some locations the project was able to reach more than one ethnicity and language group. In general, classes held with the mobile lab were in the most under-resourced areas—in communities with significant barriers that left them remarkably isolated even in a large metropolitan area. For example, at a strip mall close to the wealthiest area of Saint Paul, women came to a storefront satellite site of a large nonprofit across the street from the largest and cheapest private housing development in the city. Staff members at the organization told project workers that, in some instances, computer class or a visit to that particular office was the only time some women left their apartments. The speakers of the languages mentioned above also tended to be newcomers to Saint Paul. See figure 11.3.

Different communities required different engagement strategies: Hmong Americans represent a large share of the Saint Paul population. They did not necessarily come to computer class, in part because by 2011 generations of families had lived in Minnesota, and elders lacking computer skills were more apt to ask for help from their children and grandchildren who had grown up in Minnesota.

Thirdly, the library assumed that much time and effort would go into translating and printing curriculum for the classes. Cultural liaisons by and large interpreted existing curriculum on the fly, and many participants had low reading skills in any language and were therefore not print-oriented. The one exception was the Latino population. Project staff members theorized that other populations came to Minnesota on a more defined refugee track and had

**Figure 11.3.   Computer Class in Karen**

pathways to follow for assistance, and therefore they were inspired to come to class by word of mouth or through a trusted organizational partner. Spanish speakers came to Minnesota less often as refugees and were used to long and difficult searches for help and information. For example, flyers posted in Spanish on the right bulletin boards at the right grocery stores equaled class participation, which was definitely not the case in other communities. Participants also wanted materials in Spanish to study at home.

The library assumed that the cultural liaisons would be stable for the duration of the project. This was not the case, and managing the liaison hiring process began immediately when it became apparent that Saint Paul populations had digital literacy needs that would be met by languages other than Somali, Hmong, and Spanish. Because the liaisons were contractors, it was possible to hire more for specific classes. By the end of the project, because of community need, there were two liaisons to the Karen community, who were arriving as the most recent and quite large refugee population in Saint Paul. The project manager also taught class in English when it became apparent that there was community need in senior apartment complexes, alternative high school settings, and some job training programs.

The role of the cultural liaison was well documented in teaching the computer classes, and as the project went on it became clear that the cultural liaisons would be helpful in library buildings and in literacy programming for children and families. The library assumed that students in mobile workplace classes would equate their instructors with the library, but by and large this was not the case. Sometimes it was possible to take students on library field trips, but this was beneficial long term only if the cultural liaison had regular hours at the library.

Lastly, in the original Knight grant, success was measured by the number of classes offered (i.e., how much did the mobile Work*place* increase the library's capacity to offer digital literacy training) and the number of people attending those classes. The mobile Work*place* project surpassed the capacity-building numbers from the start, but the numbers of people attending classes fluctuated wildly from location to location and season to season. In part, these fluctuations meant that classes switched locations frequently. By and large, SPPL is accustomed to opening its doors and providing public service seven days a week, most days of the year. In partner sites the availability of partner labs, programs, and staff varied much more, and the mobile Work*place* needed to follow these varied schedules. For example, a flood at a mosque meant canceling class in Somali for several weeks. In response to the inadequacy of numbers for showing the success of the project, the project manager purposefully began collecting stories: the student who emailed at 4:30 a.m. because that's when he could get to work and practice on a computer; the women who were really excited to change their home screen savers—the computer previously being the domain of their husbands and children; the man who took a computer class and then decided if he could learn the computer he could go back to school. These stories lead to more questions: how does a teacher honor the effort of the third-shift worker who comes to class before she goes to bed in the morning? Here the library identified the most important outcome: did participants learn the skills they needed?

Because so many other schools, nonprofits, and community-based organizations were struggling with similar questions, SPPL convened a community meeting to discuss digital literacy. This meeting started with practical issues: so many students moved between organizations, shouldn't the organizations be teaching them the same beginning computer class? Fortunately, the meeting turned into a longer, community-led process, as organizations realized that they each had particular goals to accomplish through their curricula. Eventually it was determined that the community required standards for basic digital literacy. From these standards, each organization could create a curriculum. And, out of the standards grew an assessment: how does one prove to the student and to their teacher that the student has learned something? These community meetings led to the Northstar Digital Literacy Project. The Northstar Digital Literacy assessments eventually allowed mobile Work*place* students to prove to themselves and others (in the form of a certificate) that they had the skills and literacy necessary to navigate the digital world at a basic level (https://www.digitalliteracyassessment.org/).

By 2012–2013, the end of Knight Foundation funding, the program taught more than 500 classes in 23 community locations in seven languages, including English. Initially, the mobile workplace was supposed to focus on digital literacy for job skills and help people with job search and resume creation. People, whatever language they speak or cultural background, have a multitude of reasons for engaging with internet and communications technology, and most of them aren't as simple as job search. By 2012, some of the mobile workplace class offerings took place in library buildings, often because it was the easiest institutional space in the neighborhood for people to access. How could the library capitalize on the connections with audiences traditionally more difficult to reach and continue to provide digital literacy classes and early literacy programs both in the community and at the library, both in English and other languages? In 2012, the library applied for more funding to bring on the cultural liaisons as regular library staff members and to formalize the project manager's role as the community services coordinator.

With the addition of the cultural liaisons and the project manager as the community services coordinator to the library's general funding, the coordinator sought additional funding to supplement the growing needs of the community. An LSTA grant was awarded to support the computer classes and the growth of story times, which resulted from adults who continually brought their children and youth to computer classes with them. The story times for these families were facilitated by the same liaison that taught the computer classes and brought the digital literacy learners to the library for learning beyond technology. This created a model of holistic family inclusion for lifelong learning. See figure 11.4.

As the U.S. economy rose out of the recession, the needs of the community changed, and this was reflected in the computer classes. The computer classes originally meant to teach Microsoft Word and other workplace skills began to slowly see a rise in requests for financial and information literacy classes to perform tasks such as online banking and applying for passports. Families began to ask for help with creating social media accounts on Facebook and asked for suggestions on what to purchase or how to use phones and tablets.

By 2014, the African-American liaison position was created to support the population-specific needs in English in the community and was supported through additional LSTA funding. From here began African-American story time and additional programming to work with teens and young adults. A result of this LSTA grant: 37 percent of the responding participants surveyed indicated that they did not have a computer with internet access at home. The disparity of internet connection in Saint Paul homes was a wakeup call. In

**Figure 11.4.   Story Time in Amharic**

2015, SPPL applied for a Knight Foundation grant and received it to implement the "Borrow the Internet" project, which focused on providing mobile
internet access to the community along the Green Line public transit route
and Saint Paul Public School students. The Green Line route cuts through
a large community of color, specifically a historically oppressed African-
American community and several refugee and immigrant communities.

In 2015–2016, the support of the African-American cultural liaison continued through the Bremer Foundation. This liaison continued to instruct
computer classes and story times. Several community locations began
asking for computer classes in English although the primary communities attending the classes were Spanish-, Karen-, or Somali-speaking. The
intentions of these classes were to develop English language vocabulary at
the workplace that may be missed in traditional English language learning
classes. The growth of the computer classes at this point reached the adult
basic education institutions, cultural bazaars and shopping centers, and
nearby correctional facilities.

Due to the growth of the programs over time, staff members and community members have felt empowered to ask for programming outside of the
library's traditional scope. Programs and projects that emerged from engaging with these communities ranged from folk dancing to the publishing of
two books in Karen and English to writing programs and language learning
classes. See figure 11.5.

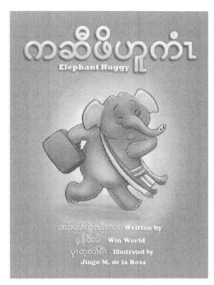

**Figure 11.5.  Books Published in Karen and English**

From 2013 through 2016, there have been 1,280 computer classes and 9,976 attendees. In the same time period, there have been 1,815 story times with an attendance of 21,911. Since the inception of the Northstar Digital Literacy Assessments (August 14, 2012), SPPL's mobile Work*place* has proctored 1,143 assessments, and of those, 793 have passed.

The success of the liaison positions has resulted in the permanent hiring of several liaisons who now have full-time positions in the library. Community services at SPPL continue to inform the library about the often-underserved needs and wishes of our most vulnerable and most resilient community members.

## REFERENCE

Dailey, Dharma, Amelia Bryne, Alison Powell, Joe Karaganis and Jaewon Chung, Broadband Adoption in Low-Income Communities (Social Science Research Council, 2010). Accessed June 20, 2017 from www.ssrc.org/publications/view/broadband-adoption-in-low-income-communities/.

# 12

## Creative Opportunity for All

### Makerspaces for Youth and Adult Workforce Populations in an Urban Setting

*Amanda Feist, Xenia Hernández, and Marika Stoloch*

Since 2012, Saint Paul Public Library (SPPL) has been providing maker activities for teens under the Createch brand, which includes weekly programming at multiple branches and daily programming five days per week at a flagship space at the Arlington Hills Community Center. This large after-school makerspace and recording studio provides a casual, welcoming atmosphere where teens can choose to hang out, play video games, and mess around with film-making, sewing, or sound production. Createch helps bridge the digital divide due to its position in the East Side neighborhood where most residents live below the poverty level.

What happens when teens age out of Createch? How do we serve adults who find themselves on the wrong side of the digital divide, shut out of career or artistic opportunities? Enter the Innovation Lab.

In October 2015, SPPL renovated the downtown branch, George Latimer Central Library (GLCL), to create the Nicholson Workforce and Innovation Center (WIN Center.) The center's mission is to serve entrepreneurs, job seekers, and creative professionals. Within the WIN Center, an adults-only makerspace called the Innovation Lab brings together patrons from these three target audiences and gives them access to technology, networking, and learning opportunities at no cost.

Both Createch and the Innovation Lab contribute to economic development by providing job and technology skills to underserved populations in a setting that integrates users from all income, skill, and cultural backgrounds. While we may consider teens underprivileged if they don't grow up with broadband access and learning to code in schools—most adults who are trying to reenter the workforce or gain new job skills grew up without these opportunities too. We welcome people into a new community where they find inspiration, expert advice, and access to equipment and resources.

## DEMOGRAPHICS AND NEED

Saint Paul, Minnesota, is a medium-size capital city with a growing minority and new immigrant population and a robust business community. SPPL is composed of 13 branches and a bookmobile, all located within the city limits, though many patrons visit from nearby suburbs and the larger twin city of Minneapolis. SPPL connects patrons to technology with both our physical spaces and our system-wide programs and services. While the library has made an effort to provide technology education and maker activities for all of our 13 branches and beyond, it is really the infrastructure investment that best demonstrates our commitment to turning libraries into a learning destination for all.

Former library director Kit Hadley traces the addition of makerspaces for youth and adult workforce populations back to the 2010 strategic plan, which re-branded SPPL as a learning destination, and a 2011 physical needs assessment of all branches that identified those in dire need of physical updates (Amanda Feist, personal communication, June 2017).

In the same year, SPPL began its physical maker initiative in the youth sphere when we received a Learning Labs planning grant for $100,000 to improve services to teens from the Institute of Museum and Library Services and the John D. and Catherine T. MacArthur Foundation. The grant funded the creation of a national cohort of digital technology spaces for teens similar to the YOUmedia Chicago Public Library spaces. Built on the philosophy of Connected Learning and letting kids hang out, mess around, and geek out (HOMAGO), with technology, we were allowed to build programs with teen input using an iterative process. The end result is Createch. It was always our intention to make the tools of learning available to patrons of all ages and to respond to workforce needs, but community needs led us to focus on youth first.

In 2010, the economy was in recession and this had a great impact on the number of job seekers and the recently unemployed looking to libraries for assistance. Adults had a very immediate need for basic services such as resume help, basic computer skills development, and English language learning. SPPL's workPLACE committee focused efforts on these basic skills through partnerships with organizations such as the Minnesota Literacy Council, Hmong American Partnership, and the AmeriCorps Community Technology Empowerment Project (CTEP). With library and partner-staff focused on helping community members find employment and assisting new immigrant populations, it took a few years for the city to stabilize enough to focus on advanced technology opportunities. By 2015, the question had become "How can we help residents get a *better* job?" rather than "How can we help people apply for unemployment and find work?" Of course, many residents still need basic computer skills, and the CTEP services members continue to provide that by teaching Northstar Digital Literacy Standards (https://www.digitalliteracy assessment.org/standards). But we wanted to show our dedication to addressing disparities in access to advanced technology in our buildings.

Currently, our two physical makerspaces are located in neighborhoods where they have great impact on some of our most under-resourced and under-privileged communities. Createch at Arlington Hills Community Center (AHCC), which is a combined building with Libraries and Parks & Recreation, attracts heavy drop-in traffic from its Payne-Phalen neighborhood. It is Saint Paul's most populous community with the highest number of residents of color (68 percent), and more than a third of its population is under 17 years of age (Compass, Payne-Phalen Neighborhood Profile, n.d.). As of May 2017, Createch at AHCC had 457 active teen members between the ages of 12 and 18, the majority at 65.9 percent identifies as male and 33.5 percent identify as female (Sprockets, 2017). See figures 12.1 and 12.2.

The Innovation Lab at George Latimer Central Library gets some drop-in traffic from neighborhood residents, but is also a destination library in the heart of downtown. It has drawn interest from across the metropolitan area, though regular visitors tend to come from closer to downtown. The active membership is composed of adults ages 19–83 (there is no upper limit), with an average of 44.5 and median age of 42. They identify as 41.4 percent female, 51.7 percent male, and 0.5 percent transgender and reflect the racial makeup of the city as a whole. See figures 12.2 and 12.3.

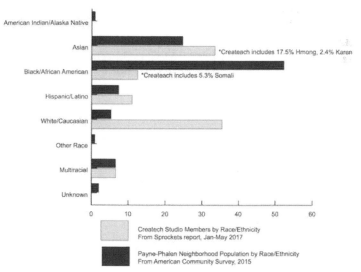

**Figure 12.1. Createch Membership vs Payne-Phalen Racial/Ethnic Makeup**
From Sprockets report, Jan.–May 2017 and American Community Survey, 2015.

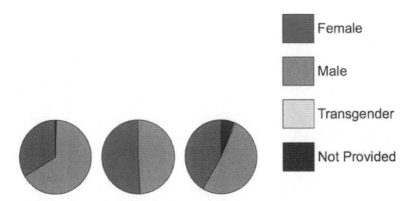

1. Createch Teen Membership by Gender, Sprockets Report, 2017.
2. City of Saint Paul Population by Gender, 2015
3. Innovation Lab Membership by Gender, Sprockets Report 2017.

**Figure 12.2.** Population by Gender Comparison of Createch, City of Saint Paul, and Innovation Lab

From Sprockets membership report 2017 and American Community Survey, 2015

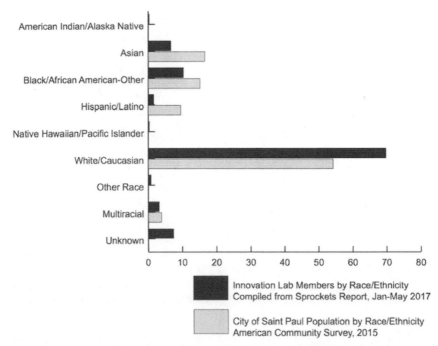

**Figure 12.3.** Innovation Lab Members vs City of Saint Paul Racial/Ethnic Makeup

Compiled from Sprockets Report, Jan.–May 2017 and American Community Survey, 2015

The most active users in the Innovation Lab illustrate how public libraries are exceptionally poised to give technological privileges to the most vulnerable. In 2017 the top three most frequent users all self-identify as patrons experiencing homelessness or staying in shelters. They check in most frequently to use laptops, followed by the recording studio and sewing machines. The top 20 visitors made up 577 of the year's 1,183 visits, and they are disproportionately more likely to be people of color. Member Valerie Roy explained the impact of our space, "I have been homeless for 6 years. I needed a place to belong and a place to work. This feels good, it adds to MY NORMALCY. The Innovation Lab is a precious gem. So much knowledge and resources here. Trying a new hobby out? Or being enterprising? So much more is being offered than any shelter or work programming that I have encountered, and I tried it all."

## HISTORY OF CREATECH STUDIO

In winter of 2011–2012, nine high school Youth Job Corps (YJC, now called Right Track) workers were hired and trained by the Science Museum of Minnesota (SMM). They formed the Teen Tech Crew (TTC) and worked in teams of three to create hands-on creative technology workshops at three sites: Rondo Community Outreach Library, Rice Street Teen Zone/Library, and the Arlington Hills Library.

At the same time, the Libraries and Parks & Recreation departments received the IMLS Learning Labs Planning grant. Initially, a goal in that grant was to create a mobile lab. We envisioned libraries and parks offering technology to out-of-school time agencies like the YMCA, church groups, and recreation centers. The advisory board developed for the grant, comprising representatives from SMM, Saint Paul Neighborhood Network, Saint Paul Public Schools, public television, and the University of Minnesota, advised against it. Instead, we focused on creating a persistent safe-space for teens that a mobile lab could complement.

In the spring of 2012, the TTC offered sporadic classes for teens using Scratch animation. During the summer months, the classes were offered weekly. As they branched out from Scratch animation—and ventured into offering a variety of "messing around" options with science, technology, and engineering—the TTC renamed their sessions "Createch Labs." Our attendance spiked. We credited this spike to the consistency of offering the technology weekly.

At the start of school, the TTC teens had to scale back to teaching once per month. Libraries and Parks decided to implement what we were learning through the IMLS grant-funded research. We started offering "hanging out" time with the mobile lab to keep a persistent teen activity offered weekly. Having consistent staff and supplementing with special events made Createch Labs a success. Attendance was high and relationships were flourishing between teen participants and staff. Teens were feeling an ownership at their library.

By November 2012, "Createch Labs" was shortened to "Createch" and we added one more site—this one in collaboration with Saint Paul Neighborhood Network (SPNN) to teach video production. Having tried intermittent programming in libraries in the past, SPNN was thrilled to have a space to try their programming biweekly, starting January 2013.

## DEFINING CREATECH

When Createch was first proposed as "a technology room for teens at the library," our initial thought was, "How are we going to lure teens to this space?" During our first grant retreat, we visited YOUmedia at Chicago Public Library and met a panel of about 15 teens who were going to answer questions about these types of spaces. With pen and paper ready, we asked, "What is the most important thing we should invest in for our spaces?" We were ready for a list of cool gadgets, trendy software, and expensive equipment.

The first girl pointed to the mentor who was the MC of the panel. "If you can get someone like Brother Mike, you should." "Yeah," the next teen said, "That's the most important thing. Good mentors." Down the row, all 15 of them had some iteration of a mentor that changed their life. Not one teen mentioned equipment. Someone in the audience raised their hand, "Yeah, but we just saw all of your computers, and games, and equipment. What out there keeps bringing you back?" An astute boy took the mic, "Yeah, that stuff is great. But really what keeps us coming back is the people." Mentors became an integral part of Createch with the relationships between mentors and teens being key to generating excitement and developing projects of interest to members.

## SPACE, EQUIPMENT, AND USAGE

Fast forward to May 2014: this was the opening week at Createch at Arlington Hills Community Center (AHCC), a brand-new building and the first shared space and staff between Libraries and Parks & Recreation. We had a couple of things going for us when it came to recruitment of teens. One, this new building was sorely needed in an under-resourced neighborhood. The library and rec center combo would bring together two populations of teens that rarely comingled. The community center was replacing a tiny Carnegie library and a rec center that was little more than an ice-skating warming house. The architects placed Createch on the bottom floor, right next to the gymnasium. We were excited about the placement—it would shield the teens from well-meaning, shushing patrons of the library and draw in teens coming or going from the gym. We didn't have to worry about attracting the teens.

In the first week, attendance was around 100 teens per day. We were excited that many teens were coming, yet we couldn't maintain the numbers. It took a bit of time to set norms and routines, to create a sense of belonging, and establish trust. Now, Createch at AHCC averages about 35 teens per day. We strive to be accessible to diverse populations and aim to attract a representative number of girls and boys to the space. Currently, the greatest concentration of members resides in the library's neighborhood. We hope to draw in youth that reflect the community where Createch is located. See figure 12.4.

One of Createch's star members and a neighborhood patron, Destiny Walker has been an active user since 2013. She led the opening-day teen advisory group in 2014 connected with Saint Paul Neighborhood Network's youth programming teams, and in spring 2017 led their efforts to secure grant funding and organize Saint Paul's first Queer Prom. Finally, she was selected to spend this past summer working as an intern through the Public Library Association's Inclusive Internship Initiative and is pursuing librarianship as a career.

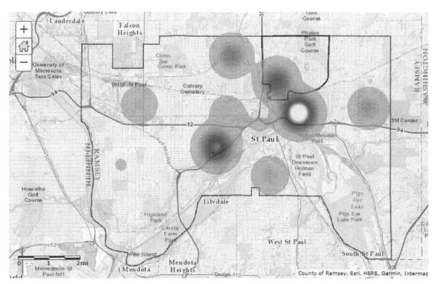

**Figure 12.4. Createch Active Membership—Area of Influence by Zip Code**
Compiled from Sprockets report, Jan.–May 2017

## STAFFING AND PARTNERSHIPS

Createch is staffed by a mixture of librarians, clerical staff, and parks workers. There are also AmeriCorps Vista and Community Technology Empowerment Program Service Members who assist with recruiting volunteers, direct service, and capacity building projects. Createch employs two Right Track teens to help staff while they gain work experience and set an example for other members. Mentors are a crucial part of engaging teens more deeply in their work and represent community members, parents, and local artists. Community Ambassadors live in the neighborhood and "are youth outreach workers who are experienced with working with Survival Based Youth and Families" (Chicago Public Library, *YOUmedia*, n.d). They are proactive in deescalating and preventing violence from entering the space and also counsel teens in crisis.

Createch developed from partnerships. Saint Paul Public Library (SPPL) had the space, staff, and administrative assistance for Createch. Saint Paul Parks and Recreation worked with us on the IMLS Learning Labs Grant and cooperates Createch at AHCC. The Science Museum of Minnesota (SMM)/ Kitty Anderson Youth Science Center trained the Createch staff and the Right Track workers who formed the Teen Tech Crew (TTC). The TTC teens lead workshops at Createch sites, help create the content, engage their peers in the activities, and reflect on what is working and what could be improved after each session. Saint Paul Neighborhood Network (SPNN) led video production programming and currently has the only Createch space that is not in a library.

We partnered with local universities, including the Playful Learning Lab at the University of St. Thomas, which connects engineering undergrads with teens in Createch sites and offers professional development to our staff. The University of Minnesota Learning Technologies Media Lab researchers also observed Createch sessions, conducted focus groups, and presented findings to our staff.

## CONNECTING WITH THE COMMUNITY

Createch quickly learned that teens needed to feel safe in a space before they were going to create anything in it. We adopted Mimi Ito's philosophy of "Hanging Out, Messing Around and Geeking Out" (Ito, 2010). Allowing teens to come into a space and hang out, play video games, and gaze at iPad screens was essential to get teens interested in coding, circuitry, and STEM activities. Mentors and teens bring their interests and passions to the space and learn from each other.

One mentor suggested that we purchase a sewing machine, and from that, we have started a sewing culture, where young men and women have learned to make their own pajama bottoms, pillows, and dresses. We've expanded with an additional sewing machine, dress forms, and a rack of donated clothes and fabric.

We've learned to measure these socioemotional targets, like whether the teens felt greeted their first time walking into Createch (92 percent did) and whether they would recommend Createch to a friend (97 percent do); 76 percent of our teens say they feel comfortable around Createch staff, and that's what keeps them coming back.

Createch continues to evolve with teen and mentor interests, keeping it fresh and relevant for the teens who consider it their second home. When asked to describe Createch in one sentence, teens responded with statements like, "very open and fun to experiment with different types of subjects," "an artistic mixing pot," and "the best thing I ever been to." One teen said, "You should go to Createch because they always have staff to support you and materials to help you." For us, there is no better review.

## HISTORY OF THE NICHOLSON
## WORKFORCE AND INNOVATION CENTER

While Createch Studio continued to grow and flourish, it was time to begin considering a permanent site for connecting adults with maker technology. The library had hosted the annual all-ages Maker Fest since 2014 and held a weekly program called Tinker Tuesdays where artists led make-and-take crafts for adults, but there was no dedicated space with access to equipment and teachers.

In 2015, the Friends of the Saint Paul Public Library raised enough funds through their capital campaign to begin a renovation of George Latimer Central Library (GLCL). Built in 1917, the library had been through several remodels and a major restoration in 2000–2002. Unfortunately, the building continued to lack sufficient infrastructure for the heavy demand created by the digital revolution. Library director Kit Hadley had a plan to transform one of the six wings into a "Workforce and Innovation Center" where services to job seekers and business owners would reside. Because the center would have a heavy focus on digital skills development, Hadley also hoped to add a makerspace to expand on the access that Createch Studio had provided. We hired a librarian who would be assigned to manage the space and work with the construction project manager and the workPLACE committee to design programming, equipment, and partnerships.

On October 5, 2015, the library closed its doors for four months during construction, and we began researching the community and its needs, as well as laying the groundwork for partnerships between the library, government entities, community organizations, and business owners. We set out to meet with other workforce centers, local economic development agencies like the Eastside Area Business Association, the Neighborhood Development Center, the Asian Economic Development Center, and the neighboring James J. Hill Center. The addition of the makerspace to construction plans required extensive research as it now involved purchasing equipment, some changes to the architectural plans, and lining up a programming schedule that addressed the new space's technology and mission.

We conducted a literature review to identify best practices in designing makerspaces in public libraries. We visited local sites with maker technology and conducted email and phone interviews with other libraries to get their advice for equipment, staff training, and services. A few notable trends emerged. In the metro area, there were no free makerspaces for adults, and none at all in Saint Paul.

Within libraries, most had some sort of membership agreement and training for both staff and patrons. Recording studios and sewing were notably popular with youth, and digitization for older adults. Makers preferred Apple computers and access to Adobe products. Soundproofing was deemed essential, while 3D printing tended to bring up feelings of frustration with the technology available not meeting patron expectations. We did decide to purchase a 3D printer, which has proved to be wise as most patrons expect a makerspace to have one as much as they expect a library to have books.

Not all advice in the research phase turned out to apply to George Latimer Central Library. Mikael Jacobsen, Learning Experiences manager at Skokie Public Library, found that he saw people using his space for their work, but not attending formal programming. "They make crowdfunding projects or are recording artists using the space for their work, but do not attend classes on video editing" (Amanda Feist, personal communication, October 2015). This greatly contrasts with what we found to be true in the Innovation Lab—where patrons are much more likely to attend planned programs instead of drop-in. Also, soundproofing was extremely expensive, and we could not reach the STC rating we desired and remain in budget. Each library is unique and should respond to the needs and characteristics of their community as they face challenges of space, environment, and political climate.

We also learned from others' mistakes, such as California State University, San Bernardino Library's attempt to create a co-working space in the library. Based in part on this article, and also the competition from a local well-known co-working space, it was decided that structured classes or project-based programming might be better choices than advertising the Innovation Lab as a "co-working space."

Construction projects always take longer than expected, especially in a 100-year-old building. Though we hoped to reopen all at once in January to align with a local Winter Carnival celebration, damage to historic plaster molding on the ceiling and a delay in soundproof doors for the study rooms pushed the grand opening of the WIN Center to March 12, 2016. All stakeholders who had been consulted during the planning of the space were invited to the opening celebration, and it was a great opportunity to establish new partnerships.

## DEFINING THE INNOVATION LAB

We didn't want the space to be a warehouse for either books or technology, but rather a unique department offering specific services to library patrons. Aligning collections, programs, and services with a unified goal was vital. Hadley and SPPL's workPLACE committee initially drafted the mission of the WIN Center as a place to offer:

• Supportive learning for underserved populations
• Free access to skills-building training
• Space for the incubation of ideas, meetings, networking, and sharing
• Entrepreneurship support when possible

We ended up doing all of the above, but shortened our mission as follows: *The Nicholson Workforce and Innovation Center serves jobseekers, entrepreneurs, and creative professionals through print and electronic resources, reference services, free training and networking opportunities and the equipment and software of the Innovation Lab.*

The mission of the Innovation Lab nests nicely into the mission of the WIN Center as a whole, which determines how we develop new services. Our festivals and crafting events serve as a networking opportunity for participants, our software classes provide job and business skills, and our equipment allows for the production of prototypes and other commercial applications. This focus has helped us articulate our value to the local community and secure partnerships with related organizations, and it has given us guidance when weighing new opportunities.

## SPACE, EQUIPMENT, AND USAGE

The Innovation Lab, on the third floor of George Latimer Central Library, is currently equipped with a laser engraver, two 3D printers, a laptop suite with 13 licenses for the full Adobe Creative Cloud, sewing machines, a serger, a vinyl cutter, a recording studio, private study rooms, a meeting/classroom space, materials for yarn crafts, and a digitization station. Patrons become members by attending a one-hour orientation, in which they sign a membership agreement, learn the rules of conduct and reserving equipment, and are introduced to the community and how they can interact with it. Members must have a library card in good standing, meaning less than $10 in fines. If they owe more than $10, we use this opportunity to explain to them they can either "read down" or "do down" their debt by reading in the library, sewing winter accessories for our Community Resource Outreach Project, or watching tutorials on Lynda.com. They then get a tour and see some equipment demonstrations, with time for questions and tinkering afterward. The member agreement collects optional demographic information and invites them to join our advisory board and get on the mailing list for our bimonthly newsletters.

Once patrons become members, they may attend classes or they may make one-on-one appointments with staff and volunteer experts. Essentially, patrons book a private meeting with a librarian or volunteer. They may already know how to use the equipment and may begin doing so without much help, or they may just want to come to our more advanced classes and networking events. We provide weekly 1–2-hour classes on the 3D printer, using Adobe Illustrator with the laser engraver, video editing with Adobe Premiere Pro, and sewing. Volunteers and staff teach the classes, so we rely on their talents in developing them. We do actively seek out skilled members to teach classes in areas we as librarians lack expertise—such as the higher-level design software and music production. Selecting programs, publicizing them, and retaining volunteers to teach is staff intensive and has required that we build a robust training program and pleasant work atmosphere.

As of December 2017, the Innovation Lab has 587 adult members ranging from homeless aspiring recording artists to inventors to job seekers brushing up on skills. That number continues to climb at a steady rate. Members are diverse in age, socioeconomic status, skill level, and cultural/racial background. By encouraging a culture of information sharing, entry-level instruction, and creative entrepreneurship, we have been able to make advanced technology accessible to all and help close the digital divide.

Innovation Lab member Eric Gjerde used our laser cutter to create poems out of paper he grew from bacteria, which were displayed at the Minnesota Center for the Book Arts. Inventor and owner of Sure Lock Packaging Rachel Kane uses our 3D printer to prototype designs such as her child-resistant packaging for medical cannabis. We have had several recording artists use the studio, including local author Lisa Lapka, who recorded the audiobook version of her children's book, *Horse in Socks*, and emerging artist Kenneth Davis, who has recorded parts of his album, *Cali Vibes, Minnesota Night*, and attended Adobe Premiere Workshops to work on his music video and marketing materials.

## STAFFING AND PARTNERSHIPS

We drafted staff that had technical aptitude or interest to be the first trained on equipment. Eight librarians, associates, specialists, and clerical workers make up the Central Tech Crew—at least one person on the crew is in the WIN Center during all open hours. They have had special training to access the database that tracks member information and attendance, and they take appointments on pieces of equipment or subject matters they have mastered. For example, two staff members are accomplished sewing instructors, while nearly everyone can get someone started on the laser engraver. Innovation Lab staff members share information about troubleshooting, local events and resources, and training opportunities at biweekly meetings. They also learn from the advisory board, which combines staff, volunteers, and patrons who tend to have expertise in some area of maker technology. The board has members from local private makerspaces and companies with ties to the local tech industry, which has resulted in useful partnerships and invitations to events.

We have been building our volunteer base and hope to increasingly be able to rely on volunteers for appointments and providing group instruction, while also offering experts compensation for their time teaching classes and leading events through contracts whenever possible. We have a formal partnership with local nonprofit Springboard for the Arts to provide classes on business skills for artists, something we hope to continue in the future. Work-study interns have also been a welcome addition, bringing youth and diversity in experience and interests. We have had one art, two engineering, and an apparel design and fashion merchandising intern. Like Createch, we also employ Right Track workers, but our employees are part of the more advanced track and can lead classes and assist patrons with operating technology.

Saint Paul had an existing Small Business Resource Center at the Rondo Community Outreach Library, and the idea was not to replicate this, but rather to expand those services that were most successful and respond to the local demand of downtown. Like the Small Business Resource Center, we partner with local economic development associations, government institutions, and nonprofits to enhance programs and services in the WIN Center. For example, we partner with a company called Joule MicroNation that provides free workshops on social media, marketing, and web design for entrepreneurs. We have partners in the city's procurement, planning, and human resources departments and work with them to advertise opportunities for job seekers and small business owners and to generally help people navigate city government. We have had very successful SCORE workshops for people starting businesses downtown while Rondo Library holds monthly workshops that include city representatives, SCORE volunteers, and LegalCORPS. We share a building with a private business library, the James J. Hill Center, and frequently share information about our programs and resources with their patrons and vice versa. Staff members also attend informal local meetings of entrepreneurs in the community to connect with inventors and artists.

The library already had a very successful partnership with AmeriCorps, through its Community Technology Empowerment Program (CTEP) and service members in five libraries, including GLCL. CTEPs teach basic computer skills classes, provide smartphone and tablet clinics, and one-to-one computer and job search assistance. Many entrepreneurs and inventors lack the necessary digital and technical skills to succeed in their field. We have observed that marketing, music production, graphic design, and technical writing are some areas where the industry standard requires high levels of fluency with complex software applications. CTEP service members, staff, interns, and volunteers all assist members as they leap over this digital divide.

## CONNECTING WITH THE COMMUNITY

While some maker technology, like 3D printing, becomes more widely available and lower in cost, others continue to be unaffordable, such as laser engraving and creative production software. Innovative technology inherently moves into obsolescence more quickly—something software companies have profited from with subscription-based pricing models. Most private spaces require membership fees, which of course is a barrier for underserved communities. There is also underrepresentation of women in makerspaces and as entrepreneurs (Bean, Farmer, and Kerr, 2015), while at SPPL our programs attract a higher percentage of people who identify as women.

Some members have told us that they left another local fee-structured space due to an unwelcoming atmosphere. The library has a strict code of patron conduct that prohibits harassment, online stalking, inappropriate remarks about race, gender identity, religion, and other characteristics that distinguishes us from many other informal hacker gatherings and digital communities (http://www.sppl.org/about/policies-and-guidelines/conduct-policy). We strive to be a safe space for teens and adults, in our makerspaces and elsewhere.

Because we decided to institute a membership system for the Innovation Lab, we have been able to collect and analyze information about who uses our space. While most regular users of the Innovation Lab live near downtown Saint Paul, we are a destination library and also attract users from across the metropolitan area. A few members outside of areas with cooperative borrowing agreements have even purchased nonresident cards for the sole purpose of accessing the lab. See figures 12.5 and 12.6.

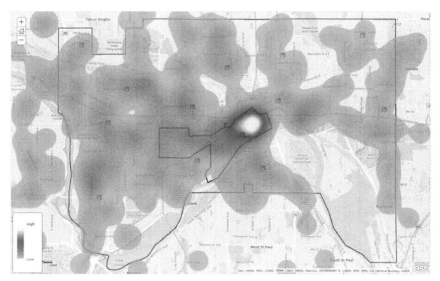

**Figure 12.5. Innovation Lab Active Membership—Area of Influence within City Limits**
Compiled from Sprockets report, Jan.–May 2017

Saint Paul's Lowertown neighborhood, only blocks from the library, is home to a vibrant artist community. They were added as a target population as they connect "maker" with "entrepreneur." While there are multiple commercial applications for the equipment in our Innovation Lab, including

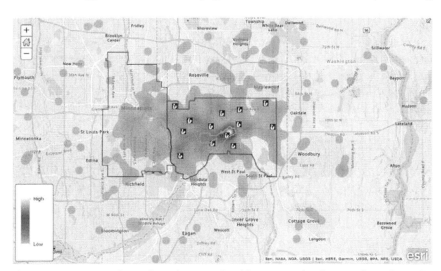

**Figure 12.6. Innovation Lab Active Membership—Area of Influence throughout the Twin Cities Metro Area**
Compiled from Sprockets report, Jan.–May 2017

prototyping and packaging, the entrepreneurs we most often see have a business selling art. We reached out to this population by handing out flyers, attending art festivals and visiting open studios in the neighborhood, and by establishing an educational partnership with a local nonprofit called Springboard for the Arts, which provides business skills education to artists. Gentrification of the neighborhood has resulted in reduced opportunities and increased costs for local artists. That combined with the inherent financial instability of art as a career leads us to consider most artists an underserved and vulnerable population.

Another underserved patron group is people experiencing homelessness. Because we do not charge money for classes or any resources beyond select consumable supplies, the Innovation Lab is accessible for these users. It is difficult to track how many members may be experiencing homelessness, but we know from conversation that they do use our space. A member experiencing homelessness travels from a shelter in Minneapolis several times a week to the Innovation Lab. She uses the recording studio to produce music, and in the process she is learning basic digital literacy skills like file management and advanced skills like sound editing and Photoshop. In the winter of 2016–2017, lab volunteers began a service project in which they made warm headbands with donated fleece fabric for distribution at the library's weekly Community Resource Outreach Program (CROP) for people experiencing homelessness. CROP brings together various local nonprofit and social service agencies for drop-in consultations and services along with coffee and cookies every Wednesday afternoon. The headbands were not only practical, but also became a conversation piece that informed patrons about the sewing machines and instructors available in the Innovation Lab. Several CROP clients became lab members and learned how to mend clothes, use our recording studio, and connect with family members through our Skype-enabled laptops.

As our membership continues to grow we will continually assess our membership to make sure it reflects the local community. We know that maintaining and seeking out new relationships with community partners will help us stay relevant to all makers.

## ADVICE FROM CREATECH AND THE INNOVATION LAB

Responsiveness to the local community was vital for the planning process. For both locations we spend much of our planning process visiting other sites and actively seeking input from potential users. In Createch, equipment is purchased to supplement teen and mentor interests—the teens and mentors drive the activity, not Createch leadership. Great care is taken to maintain a casual but safe atmosphere with staff and mentors who can quickly adapt to new ideas, interests, and issues.

At George Latimer Central Library, the Innovation Lab location is such that drop-in services will never be as popular as events and classes due to the nature of the location and patron interests. By continuously assessing demographics and attendance and collecting feedback at programs and through the Advisory Board; we identify gaps and provide tangible results to our patrons. While we certainly cannot afford to do everything our patrons would like us to do, we implement a high percentage of program requests and often encourage our community members to take the lead on projects we don't have time for or can't afford, which has led to more volunteer engagement.

With both Createch and the Innovation Lab, we were also given great freedom by our funders—allowing us to experiment, create our own frameworks, and put power(ful) tools in the hands of children and elders alike. We take care to analyze member bases and usage statistics to reach our internal goals, but we are not required to serve particular populations or provide specific programs by private funders or sponsors.

## LOOKING TO THE FUTURE

Since Createch Studio and the Innovation Lab opened, makerspaces have been popping up all over the city, in schools, and other library systems. Representatives from countless libraries have visited in the planning process for their own makerspaces for youth and adults, with Createch seeing more visitors in the educational realm who already know what a makerspace is. Visitors to the Innovation Lab are often visiting from the private and economic development sectors, although local library systems and schools have also approached the space for advice.

Since opening, new member orientation—held four times monthly for first-time visitors—continues to attract an average of 8–10 attendees per session, which tells us that we have not yet reached our entire potential user base. We see this as evidence that there truly was a need for adults to have access to publicly funded technology, and we expect this trend will continue to grow. The Innovation Lab also welcomes patrons who have previously been members of private makerspaces but left because of a lack of training or other issues that made them feel unwelcome there. Createch is strategically located in an area where many residents don't have reliable access to free after-school enrichment programs that are giving them the workforce skills they will need. Saint Paul Public Library has made making everyone feel welcome a core part of its brand, and we find that people generally have a positive attitude toward libraries even if they are not regular users. By continuing to seek out new partners and maintaining the relationships we have, we strengthened our community's knowledge of our resources.

Participants at both the Createch Studio and the Innovation Lab are engaged in creative, productive activities and are strengthening our economy. We have begun to capture their successes by telling their stories in newsletters, on social media, in print promotions and reports. We hope to elevate the technical skills of our patrons in such a way that their achievements demonstrate the usefulness of our programs.

The Saint Paul Public Library's mission is to connect people in Saint Paul with the imperative and the joy of learning through a lifetime. With our Createch Studio and the Innovation Lab, we have sparked much joy and learning through technology, for both staff and patrons of all ages.

## REFERENCES

Bean, Vanessa, Nicole M. Farmer, and Barbara A. Kerr. "An Exploration of Women's Engagement in Makerspaces." *Gifted & Talented International* 30 (2015): 61.
Chicago Public Library. YOUmedia. n.d. www.chipublib.org/programs-and-partner ships/youmedia (accessed December 2017).
Compass, Wilder Research–Minnesota. Payne-Phalen Neighborhood Profile. 2011–2015. www.mncompass.org/profiles/neighborhoods/st-paul/payne-phalen (accessed December 2017).
Franklin, Joel A. Community Ambassadors Initiative Final Report 2016. Saint Paul: Hallie Q. Brown Community Center, 2016.
Hadley, Kit, interview by Amanda Feist. Personal Communication with Saint Paul Public Library Director (June 2017).
Innovation Lab. *Innovation Lab Newsletter* (November–December). Saint Paul: Saint Paul Public Library, 2017.
Itō, Mozuko. *Hanging Out, Messing Around, and Geeking Out: Kids Living and Learning with New Media*. Cambridge, MA: MIT Press, 2010.
Jacobsen, Mikael, interview by Amanda Feist. Personal communication with Learning Experiences Manager at Skokie Public Library (October 2015).
Saint Paul Public Library. Library Conduct Policy. April 2017. www.sppl.org/about /policies-and-guidelines/conduct-policy (accessed December 2017).
Sprockets, CitySpan. "Createch Site Report January-May 2017." Saint Paul, 2017.
The Standards. n.d. www.digitalliteracyassessment.org/standards (accessed December 2017).

# 13

## Learning from Our Community

### Using an Assessment Tool to Meet Patrons at the Point of Need

*Amy Honisett, Gloria Jacobs, Judy Anderson,*
*Jill Castek, Cindy Gibbon, and Matthew Timberlake*

**M**ultnomah County Library is dedicated to meeting our patrons at their point of need. As technology training needs evolve, the library's programs adapt. In order to understand the changing needs of our community, the library strives to understand how people use technology and to identify modes of support that will help empower patrons in their use of technology for enjoyment and to improve their lives. To gain that understanding, the library partnered with researchers to administer an online assessment of digital problem-solving skills.

### WHO WE ARE

Multnomah County Library is a public library serving Multnomah County, Oregon. The county comprises 799,766 people across 431 square miles. The service area includes Central Library in downtown Portland, reaches into the Portland suburbs and includes the smaller cities of Gresham, Fairview, Wood Village, Maywood Park, and Troutdale.

The median age in Multnomah County is 36.5, but 14 percent of the county's population is 62 years or older. Most of the population of Multnomah County has graduated from high school and almost half (41.3 percent) have attained a bachelor's degree or higher. While the median household income is $59,000, 15.7 percent of the county's population lives in poverty. The rate of unemployment in Multnomah County is 4 percent. In 2015, 16,344 people were counted as living on the streets, in transitional housing, or "doubled up," sharing the housing of others due to economic hardship (Kristina Smock Consulting, 2015: 9).

Multnomah County Library's work is driven by our mission, "Empowering our community to learn and create." This mission is supported by priorities that guide service:

- We reflect and serve a diverse community.
- We enable creation and learning.
- We champion reading.
- We build digital literacy.
- We reimagine library services and spaces.

To fulfill our commitment to these priorities, the library reaches out into the community, as well as offering relevant programs and services inside the library walls. Multnomah County Library supports digital skill building and the acquisition of digital literacy in a number of important ways.

Multnomah County Library is part of the local Digital Inclusion Network, a network of more than 80 organizations including local government, internet service providers, community-based organizations, and nonprofits. The Digital Inclusion Network works to forward the goals of digital equity in our community, including access to affordable high-speed internet and devices, access to culturally specific training and support, and fostering a public policy framework that supports digital inclusion. MCL is part of a larger network of organizations nationally who work collaboratively toward shared aims promoting digital equity.

In 2016 the library hosted a Digital Inclusion Fellow, sponsored by the Nonprofit Technology Network (NTEN) and Google Fiber. The Fellow, Charly Eaton, partnered with a number of community organizations to teach basic computer classes. Participation in the classes allowed students to earn a free computer from a local nonprofit, Free Geek.

In addition to these large initiatives, the library is dedicated to meeting our patrons at their point of need. As technology training needs evolve, the library's programs adapt. While basic computer classes are consistently well attended, individualized assistance has also become increasingly important as people gain access to mobile technology.

## MULTNOMAH COUNTY LIBRARY CLASSES

There is a clear desire for technology training in the county. Last year, the library offered 1,434 classes, with 7,104 people attending. These classes are well received; 98 percent of people responding to an evaluation rated them "excellent" or "good," and 97 percent who responded to an evaluation indicated that they learned something new.

These classes bring together people from all sorts of backgrounds, who come to class for all sorts of different reasons. This diversity brings opportunity to learn from each other, along with the challenges inherent in meeting a variety of needs. To serve this wide range of needs, the library offers a variety of classes for beginners. The classes are intended to help students get started, so they can continue learning on their own. This means that the library offers classes focused on mousing and keyboarding skills for people who have never used a computer before, as well as programming classes to help students who are curious about what it means to be a programmer.

While evaluations show that library computer training is effective for many or most students, we may be missing part of the community. Research from the Programme for the International Assessment of Adult Competencies (PIAAC) shows that adults of all ages in the United States are less able to problem solve in digital environments than those in many other countries (OECD *Skills Matter*, 2016: 22). Not just older people, but also young people struggle to solve problems in an online environment (OECD, 2015: 46).

These findings have personal and workforce implications. Internationally, workforce participation rates and wages are lower among adults who report having no experience in using digital devices than those who have basic problem-solving skills using digital devices (OECD, 2015: 63–66). The Pew Research Center reports a "nearly 20 percentage-point difference in the incidence of personal learning in the past 12 months between those who have both smartphones and home broadband and those who have one but not both kinds of connectivity. The gap is even greater than that for those with neither smartphones nor home broadband connections" (Pew, 2016). People who are more connected engage in more personal and professional learning than those who have less access to technology, which could demonstrate an opportunity gap for those who have less experience solving problems online.

## A RESEARCH COLLABORATION

In 2015, Multnomah County Library partnered with researchers to examine adult patrons' digital problem solving. Together, the partnership was awarded a $500,000 Institute for Museum and Library Services (IMLS) National Leadership Research Grant. This three-year effort examined patrons' digital skills quantitatively by exploring general trends and qualitatively by analyzing the range of skills, strategies, and dispositions involved in digital problem solving across different contexts. This research was designed to learn how to improve library practices, programs, and services for adult patrons, especially economically vulnerable and socially isolated adults, seniors, English learners, and people lacking basic digital literacy skills. Through this research, Multnomah County Library (MCL), digital literacy researchers, and community partners created a bridge to digital equity and inclusion for traditionally excluded members of the community.

The goals of this project were established to measure patron skills in areas the library can change, if needed. The project would help determine whether or not library patrons could actually use the electronic resources provided at the library: databases, e-books, streaming music, and online class registration, and whether the technology training offered at the library is at the right level, covering the appropriate competencies. This measurement is an important way to support equity in the community by allowing us to focus our efforts on learning how to support patrons who need to gain digital skills and who may rely upon the library for access to technology.

## ASSESSING PROBLEM SOLVING IN TECHNOLOGY-RICH ENVIRONMENTS

The research group proposed to use an online tool developed by Education Services Online (ESO) to administer the "Problem Solving in Technology Rich Environments" (PSTRE) survey developed by the Programme for the International Assessment of Adult Competencies of the Organization for Economic Cooperation and Development (OECD). Digital problem solving draws on an individual's ability to engage in finding information, assess reliability, reason about sources, organize and transform information, and use online tools to create and communicate ideas (PIAAC Expert Group, 2009). However, these higher level thinking skills can be difficult to learn without support (Metzger, Flanagin, and Nekmat, 2014), which may come from school or work or, for those who are not able or who would prefer not to access support via those channels, from the library.

The PSTRE is a valid and reliable scenario-based tool (NCES, 2012). It is made up of nine multi-stem constructed response items that directly assess a person's ability to use digital technology, communication tools, and networks to acquire and evaluate information, communicate with others, and perform practical tasks in personal, work-related, and community contexts. PSTRE represents a domain of competence where digital skills meet cognitive skills. It includes the ability to accomplish tasks like organizing information, using digital tools to find and communicate information, applying criteria to comparison shop online, filling out forms—the skills library staff help patrons with every day. These skills may be taken for granted by those who have regular and easy access to technology, which in turn allows them to build skills through use and practice.

Having PSTRE skills is not the same as having computer skills. While the ability to problem solve online relies upon foundational digital skills like mousing and keyboarding, PSTRE includes cognitive dimensions not required when simply manipulating computer hardware. These dimensions are set out in the PIAAC framework:

- setting and monitoring progress
- planning
- acquiring and evaluating information
- using information

"The first PIAAC problem-solving survey focuses on the abilities to solve problems for **personal**, **work**, and **civic** purposes by setting up appropriate goals and plans and accessing and making use of information through computers and computer networks" (OECD, 2012: 47–49). The assessment organizes scores ranging from 0 to 400. These scores are then broken into four levels, with below level one representing the most basic level and level three representing the most advanced level.

**Level 1 (241–290)**: The task is performed in a single and familiar environment and the goal is explicitly stated in operational terms. Solving the problem requires a relatively small number of steps and the use of a restricted range of operators and does not demand a significant amount of monitoring across a large number of actions. This level of competency is illustrated by the ability to sort emails into pre-existing folders, using given criteria.

**Level 2 (291–340)**: The task requires switching between two different applications and involves multiple steps and operators. It also requires some amount of monitoring. Making use of the available tools greatly facilitates identifying the relevant entries. This level of competency is illustrated by the ability to respond to a request by locating information in a spreadsheet and emailing it to the requestor.

**Level 3 (341–400)**: The task involves multiple applications, a large number of steps, a built-in impasse, and the discovery and use of ad hoc commands in a novel environment. The test-taker has to establish a plan and monitor its implementation in order to minimize the number of conflicts. In addition, the test-taker has to transfer information from one application (e-mail) to another (a room-reservation tool). This level of competency is illustrated by the ability to manage requests to reserve a meeting room using a reservation system, discover a scheduling conflict, and email a decline of the request (OECD Survey of Adult Skills, 2016: 73).

These skills are not just "nice to have"; they are necessary for individuals to flexibly employ to engage in almost every aspect of modern life and make it possible to access a range of information, interact with public services, communicate with friends, engage in political activities. Moreover, they are essential for success in a workplace or school environment. However, in the United States adults lag behind their international peers in the skills required to thrive online.

The PIAAC assessment is designed to measure the test-takers' skills in literacy, numeracy, and problem solving in technology-rich environments. The Education and Skills Online assessment tool is designed so the test-taker must score sufficiently high in the literacy section to continue on to the PSTRE assessment. To avoid collecting data that would not be used and so that test-takers would not need to spend the extra time it would take to complete the literacy and numeracy components of the assessment, the research team developed a principled way to adapt the assessment tool to allow an individual to complete only the PSTRE component.

We also adapted the original PIAAC background questionnaire. Our adapted questionnaire mirrored the demographic questions found on PIAAC's background questionnaire, but our version was abbreviated and specifically designed to collect data that would inform our research. Our questionnaire included response options related to age, educational attainment, and employment status. We designed library-related questions, to determine whether a test-taker's score related to the ability to use various library services. We also believed the background questionnaire would serve as a proxy for the literacy component of the ESO assessment; if the potential test-taker was able to read and complete the background survey, we believed they would have demonstrated sufficient literacy skills to take the PSTRE assessment. Since the PSTRE assessment required that individuals could use a mouse to highlight, copy, and paste text on a screen, we included an item on our questionnaire to assess those prerequisite skills. If individuals could not independently highlight, copy, and paste, they were not invited to take the PSTRE assessment as part of our study.

## Staff Pilot

Before rolling out this assessment to patrons, we wanted to get staff input and buy-in. By asking staff to take the assessment, we hoped we could interrupt difficulties in advance, discover the best ways to frame the assessment for our patrons, and be prepared for any potential problems. We also wanted to give staff a chance to see the assessment so that they could answer patron questions.

We asked staff to take the assessment using their own skills, rather than pretending they were patrons, but to keep the patron perspective in mind as they worked through the test. As staff completed the assessment, we asked them to complete short surveys to provide feedback on the assessment experience and on the background survey. While we would not be able to change the assessment, feedback from staff would help us frame the assessment for our patrons.

We asked staff about the assessment process: whether it was too long, what part was most challenging, and whether they see a relationship between the problem-solving skills in the assessment and the way patrons solve problems in the library. The responses we received were insightful. For example, in response to whether there is a relationship between the assessment and patron problem solving, staff members wrote,

> Yes, because there are many processes in wayfinding and research in libraries that require you to use several skills at once. And the web and email are hard enough for many people, but when you add in the complexities of the library web site and catalog, it is that much more complicated (Honisett, survey response, November 9, 2015).

> It assesses whether the patron has learned how to look at the screen. When the setup is too new, one focuses on what one knows & the rest just swims in the distance. If one has familiarity, one can look for other possibilities (Honisett, survey response, November 9, 2015).

As a result of what we learned from the pilot, we were able to improve our protocol. In particular, we learned that we should emphasize to the test-takers that the assessment interface will not look familiar.

We also learned that the score report generated by the assessment tool is intimidating and dense, so we created a new one using plain language and adding white space. We included information about taking classes at the library so that the test-taker would not feel helpless if their score was not as high as they would have liked.

During the staff pilot, staff expressed concern that our patrons might have trouble deciphering the highly academic language used in the Spanish language assessment. Because of this input, and the input of a bilingual librarian on our team, we decided not to offer the assessment in Spanish.

## Finding Participants

*In the Library*

We set up a table with laptops in the entrance to two libraries and asked people to take the background survey as they walked in. We soon discovered that many people were not interested, and those who did take the background survey did not have time to take the assessment at that time. Later, we scheduled our time in the library to coincide with story times, and we asked the youth librarian to promote the project. This produced better results, and we let people who took the background survey know that we might contact them later to invite them to take a longer assessment, with a financial incentive.

Of the 98 people who took the background survey in the library, we invited 65 to take the assessment. Our criteria for inviting participation were: 1) was the participant willing to take the assessment, and 2) did they have the prerequisite skills to use the mouse to highlight, copy, and paste independently? Most of those people took the assessment at home, rather than coming back into the library. We developed brief instructions and emailed them, along with the code to access the assessment. We tracked these codes on a spreadsheet, following up with patrons who had either started the assessment but not finished or who had not accessed the assessment after one week. Assessments that were not used were reassigned to different patrons.

*At the Reference Desk*

We soon realized that spending time in library locations soliciting participation was very time intensive for a low return. We created handbills promoting the project:

*The library needs your help!*

We want to make sure our resources work for everyone.

**You can help!**

Take this 10 minute survey: http://bit.ly/mcltechsurvey

Some people will be invited back to take a longer assessment of their digital problem solving skills. People who take that assessment will be compensated $20.

Thank you for taking part! Your input will help us improve our services.

We asked reference staff to hand these out to patrons who approached the reference desk or who they encountered in the library. We also created a larger sign to post near our public access computers and in our computer labs.

*Email Newsletter*

Multnomah County Library's email newsletter reaches 46,000 people. We included a solicitation in that newsletter using similar language to the handbill, emphasizing that this is an opportunity to help the library improve services.

## Participation

We tracked our promotional efforts using bit.ly links. While signs were not effective, we found that asking for help from reference staff was extremely effective: 429 people accessed the link we included on the handbill provided at the reference desk. The next most effective promotional strategy was asking volunteer instructors to promote the assessment during one-on-one technology training; this produced 11 interactions.

As we analyzed the results of our background survey, we noticed that our pool of potential test-takers had many characteristics in common. Providing the option to take the background survey at home and gathering information from people who either received the library's email newsletter or who approached the reference desk had resulted in contact with a disproportionate number of people who are well educated. Our efforts in the library locations had also resulted in a large number of younger women participating, as we had focused on connecting with people leaving story time, most of whom were young mothers.

## Outreach

We were aware that we would not be able to attain a representative sample of Multnomah County Library patrons. However, in order to make the sample look more like the community, we decided to focus our promotional and outreach efforts on the community of people around the library experiencing homelessness or who qualified as low income.

Because we were trying to reach people who may not have access to an internet connected computer, we booked time for "assessment labs" in the downtown library's computer lab. In order to facilitate the process, we decided to allow anyone who showed up to take both the background survey and the assessment. This was to avoid asking people to come back twice. Based on our previous experience recruiting patrons, we did not anticipate many people would participate. Therefore, we made the sessions first-come, first-served.

We asked library staff to bring handbills to a local homeless shelter and a low income apartment during library outreach. We also informed a local nonprofit neighborhood center and social service agency about our project.

Our first assessment lab was scheduled to begin two hours after the library opened. A group of five or six potential participants were waiting at the front door at opening, asking how they could ensure a spot in the lab. Patrons continued to arrive until the designated time for the lab. The computer lab can only accommodate nine people at a time, so we tried to let participants enter in the order they arrived. The patrons were mostly self-organizing, although we did have to turn some people away once we had run out of codes and incentive funds that day.

During the assessments we administered in the lab, we observed test-takers helping each other. These interactions seemed to happen very naturally. There was a feeling of camaraderie in the room, and the test-takers seemed eager to help each other. This mutual support reflects what library trainers see during classes. Collaboration among students is a great way to support learning. We also wanted to learn more about how working together changes the way people problem solve in technology-rich environments.

## A New Approach

Our initial analysis of the background survey and PSTRE data revealed scoring patterns similar to the national data, but this finding was insufficient for our needs. We wanted to learn more than the ESO assessment tool could teach us. Rather than just discovering the level at which our patrons fell within a range of scores, we wanted to learn how our patrons leverage the skills and experience they have and how those skills translate to use of library resources. In order to gain a richer perspective, we developed a qualitative research approach that included working directly with patrons as they took the assessment and completed five tasks that require use of the library website.

As we developed the five library tasks, we mapped them to the PSTRE framework to ensure that they were consistent with what was being tested by the PSTRE assessment. For example,

1. Find the Overdrive e-book *My Beloved World* by Sonia Sotomayor. Check it out and open it so that you can read it on your desktop.
   a. Setting goals, monitoring progress
      i. Patron determines: "Did my search work appropriately? Do I need to begin again?"
      ii. How does the patron respond to unexpected events, impasses?
   b. Planning, self-organizing
      i. Does the patron think about where/how to search before beginning?
      ii. Does the patron seek appropriate places to search on the website?
      iii. Does the patron use facets to narrow search?
   c. Acquiring and evaluating information

      i.   Can the patron focus attention on the appropriate section of the website? Does the patron understand the difference between the right and left side results?

     ii.   Does the patron determine which link to click, or does the patron just click the first result?

    iii.   Does the patron use the information provided in the item-level description to make a determination of appropriateness?

  d.  Using information

      i.   Can the patron check out the material? (Does the patron know where to go?)

     ii.   Can the patron determine how to open the book and read it on the desktop?

Patrons were invited to a comfortable, yet businesslike environment and worked in pairs or with a researcher. We asked the test-takers to think aloud about their process, what they were attending to on the screen, and their decisions about where to navigate and which resources to use as they worked. At times, we asked questions to help us understand their process. We used screen capture software to record what they were doing and saying as they completed the assessment tasks. When patrons seemed to reach an impasse with any of the tasks, one of us would step in to provide just enough support to help them at their point of need. At the end of the session, we asked the test-takers to talk about their experience of the assessment and the library tasks. Thus, the session served to support the patrons as well as providing us with vital data.

## A Learning Analytic Tool

In order to understand how the test-takers moved through the ESO assessment and the library tasks, a researcher from our team developed a tool we called a "learning analytic tool" to indicate where the test-taker falls within a spectrum of observable skills. The observable skills we looked for include the four cognitive dimensions described in the PSTRE framework, along with one additional dimension, pragmatic knowledge. We defined pragmatic knowledge as the level of familiarity the test-taker has with similar interfaces and why those interfaces are used in everyday life. By looking for the application of pragmatic knowledge, we hoped to determine whether the test-taker's facility aligned with the opportunities afforded to that person to use technology.

For each cognitive dimension, we indicated with how much independence the test-taker completes the task, from complete independence, to a prolonged attempt that requires direct guidance from one of the research team in order to complete the task. We also indicated if the test-taker was unable to complete the task and gave up. For example,

- The participant exhibits the ability to assess whether the strategy used worked as expected.
- The participant starts over or adjusts the strategy as needed.
- The participant establishes and applies criteria for making decisions.
- When prompted, the participant is able to determine whether the strategy worked.
- The participant needs prompting or encouragement to start over or adjust the strategy.
- The participant initially has unclear criteria for making decisions but is able to do so with prompting.

## Results

While we did not assess a representative sample of Multnomah County residents, 464 people completed our background survey, 197 completed the ESO assessment, and 26 went through the observational protocols with the library tasks. Most of the people in our sample were older than 24, and most of them were unemployed. People who were employed tended to achieve higher scores on the assessment. See figure 13.1.

More than half of those who took the assessment have a four-year college or university degree or beyond. Those test-takers who had completed more than secondary education tended to score higher than those who had not gone

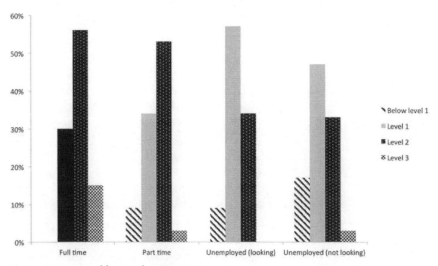

Figure 13.1.   Level by Employment Status

beyond high school. How and where a person accesses the internet most often may also affect their ability to problem solve online. Those test-takers who indicated that they access the internet most often from the library tended to score lower on the assessment than those who access the internet most often from work or home. The test-takers who indicate that they access the internet most often from a mobile device tended to score lower than those who do not access the internet most often from a mobile device.

## Self-Perception

Based on our question:
   When I'm doing something online

- I can usually figure it out
- I can figure it out but it's really hard
- I almost always get stuck

we learned that those test-takers who score below level one and those who score at level three tend to have an accurate perception of their online skills (most who score below level one indicate they have difficulty, all who scored at level three indicate they can usually figure it out). Those test-takers who fall into the levels one and two score bands may be less certain of their online skills, or they might recognize that their skills depend on the level of complexity of the task they are attempting to complete online.

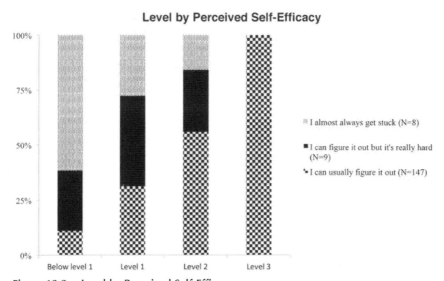

Figure 13.2.   Level by Perceived Self-Efficacy

We recognize that online problem-solving abilities are multi-faceted, context specific, and too complex to measure with one simple score. Instead, one's ability to complete a task online may depend on a number of factors, including how high stakes the problem is in the problem solver's life, the confidence with which the problem solver approaches the task, and the familiarity of the application the problem solver is using to complete the task.

Analysis using the learning analysis tool allowed us to acknowledge the importance of collaboration and reassurance as the test-taker works to complete a task. We observed some test-takers become unstuck once the researcher offered minimal assistance or encouragement. This tool also allowed the research team to understand online problem solving as fluid, rather than a static or innate competence. The ability to complete a task may be dependent on scaffolding, familiarity with the interface, emotional readiness to complete the task, fatigue, and a set of attitudes we termed "stances."

## PROBLEM-SOLVING STANCES

Based on analysis of our observational data, we identified several *stances*, or ways of approaching problem solving in a technology-rich environment. These stances include the following emerging categories. We are continuing to refine our insights through a final round of data collection and analysis.

**The Procedural Problem Solver** moves through a problem step by step and needs help when experiencing something that cannot be tackled using a step-by-step procedure.

**The Schematic Problem Solver** draws heavily from past experience or schema. A person who adopts this stance is successful as long as his/her past experiences are helpful to draw on. A schematic problem solver struggles when the knowledge gained from past experiences is insufficient to solve the problem at hand. For example, if the resources available differed from those the individual is used to using or features within those resources operated differently.

**The Exploratory Problem Solver** examines resources, clicks through menus, and investigates the digital terrain. The exploratory problem solver is willing to try different approaches to accomplish the task, shifting strategies when one approach might not yield the anticipated result. However, an individual with an exploratory stance might need help returning to the original goal if he/she spends too much time exploring or gets lost in the exploration.

**The Learn through Experience Problem Solver** takes what was learned in a previous task and is able to apply it to a new task. Learning through experience involves recognizing that the digital resources one uses in a certain context can be useful in other settings as well. This problem solver might need help if the two circumstances are not as similar as was thought.

**The Good Enough Problem Solver** does enough to complete the task but is not concerned with being thorough nor double-checking his/her work. He/she may go ahead with the first almost right answer they find, but not examine all the resources to determine if a better answer could be found. Thus, this type of problem solver might miss important information needed to complete the task fully and need helps to be able to determine what is most important to pay attention to.

**The Flexible Problem Solver** does not get frustrated when the approach being used does not work; instead, this type of problem solver creates a work-around. However, problems may arise when the problem solver gets focused on the work-around and misses the nuances of the task.

An individual may first employ one stance to approach a problem and then adopt another stance later down the road. These stances are fluid and context dependent. A problem solver may attempt to solve a problem using past experiences to inform the strategy, demonstrating the schematic problem-solving stance, but if that approach does not lead to a solution, a successful problem solver can switch to a procedural or exploratory problem-solving stance. A problem solver who prefers the exploratory problem-solving stance may shift to a schematic or procedural problem-solving stance when failing to solve a problem using the exploratory strategy. Because skills alone cannot account for the entire terrain of digital problem-solving competency, stances provide a way to teach patrons to adopt, learn, and employ flexible approaches to problem solving within an ever-changing digital landscape that will evolve as new tools and technologies emerge in our digital world.

## WHAT DOES THIS MEAN FOR LIBRARIES?

The results of our background survey demonstrate that patrons who use the library website find it easy to use. However, we also see that many people who responded to the survey do not use the library website to accomplish basic information-seeking tasks like finding health information, getting help with a resume, or even finding a library program or class. This may be because our patrons are not aware of the resources the library offers, but it might be due to the level of problem-solving skills needed to successfully navigate the site.

As we watched test-takers move through the library tasks we designed for the observational protocol, we noticed impasses and redirections. During our analysis of these observations, we became aware of places in which the library site and the language used on the site differ from online spaces more familiar to the test-taker. We watched one test-taker struggle to "find a résumé help session at a time and location convenient for you." The library defines "résumé help" as a program or event, but we saw a patron define it as a service and have difficulty completing the task when he was unable to find "résumé help" in our list of services. The patron not only defined a "service" in a different way than library staff, he did not recognize that the list of services on the library website was not a comprehensive list of everything the library has to offer. Similarly, we observed a test-taker attempt to use a filtered search field to refine his results, but he did not click the "apply" button, so the facet was never applied.

It may be important to address our community's skill levels from both ends. Not only do we need to find ways to support our patrons in becoming more adept online problem solvers, we also need to take steps to ensure that our online resources are accessible by patrons with low PSTRE abilities. We can take steps to:

- use plain language on the library website and in training material;
- assess the usability of the library website among community members with a wide variety of educational and employment backgrounds, as well as with people who usually access the internet using a mobile device; and
- let vendors know we want electronic resources to be easy to use.

In library classes and training sessions, perhaps we should emphasize collaboration and flexibility, traits that can help problem solvers overcome impasses. Offering many ways for patrons to learn about technology may help respond to a variety of approaches to learning. Offering handouts, online tutorials, in-person classes, and individualized assistance could help move toward training that not only helps our patrons learn the answers to their technology questions, but also improves their problem-solving skills. The ability to access training appropriate to one's current stance toward learning might help the learner build the skills needed to become a more flexible and self-directed learner.

## REFERENCES

Kristina Smock Consulting. 2015. *2015 Point-In-Time Count of Homelessness in Portland/Gresham/Multnomah County, Oregon.*
Metzger, M. J., A. J. Flanagin, and E. Nekmat. (2014). Optimistic biases in online credibility evaluation among parents and children. Paper presented at the annual meeting of the International Communication Association, Seattle, WA.

National Center for Educational Statistics (NCES). 2012. *Problem Solving in Technology-Rich Environments Domain.* Available at https://nces.ed.gov/surveys /piaac/problem-solving.asp.

OECD (Organisation for Economic Co-Operation and Development). 2012. *Literacy, Numeracy and Problem Solving in Technology-Rich Environments: Framework for the OECD Survey of Adult Skills.* Paris: OECD Publishing.

OECD (Organisation for Economic Co-Operation and Development). 2015. *Adults, Computers and Problem-Solving: What's the Problem?* Paris: OECD Publishing.

OECD (Organisation for Economic Co-Operation and Development). 2016. *Skills Matter: Further Results from the Survey of Adult Skills.* Paris: OECD Publishing.

OECD (Organisation for Economic Co-Operation and Development). 2016. *The Survey of Adult Skills: Reader's Companion, Second Edition*, OECD Skills Studies. Paris: OECD Publishing.

Pew Research Center. 2016. *Lifelong Learning and Technology.*

PIAAC Expert Group in Problem Solving in TechnologyRich Environments. "PIAAC Problem Solving in Technology-Rich Environments: A Conceptual Framework." *OECD Education Working Papers*, no. 36 (2009). OECD Publishing. http://dx.doi .org/10.1787/220262483674.

# Index

# About the Editor and Contributors

## EDITOR

**Lauren Comito** has been working to level the playing field for New York City library users for over a decade, currently as the Neighborhood Library supervisor at the Mill Basin Branch of the Brooklyn Public Library. In her previous work as the Job & Business Academy Manager at Queens Library, she developed a team that has helped hundreds of people find employment opportunities. She created the Where in Queens mobile website as a development on the ideas put forth by ZenDesk and LinkSF, with whom she laid the groundwork for a partnership while she was presenting at SXSW Interactive. Lauren has logged hundreds of hours training people how to use technology to improve their lives and job opportunities.

Lauren is also very invested in the library ecosystem, serving in numerous capacities in ALA (Council, Committee on Library Advocacy) and in the New York Library Association (President Leadership & Management Section, chair of the Communication Committee). She is the chair of the Board of Urban Librarians Unite as well as being a founding member of the organization. She started ULU's Urban Librarians Conference and has organized this highly regarded conference for four years with speakers and attendees from across the country.

Lauren Comito was awarded a *Library Journal* Mover & Shaker award for her work with tech training and job readiness. Her workgroup received the 2015 Gale Cengage Award for Excellence in Reference & Adult Library Services for the Where in Queens project. She is regularly asked to speak at regional and national conferences on topics of tech, tech training, women in leadership, cross generational management, and library advocacy.

## CONTRIBUTORS

**Davis Erin Anderson** is community engagement manager at Metropolitan New York Library Council, where she works to organize (and sometimes lead) workshops, conferences, and other events that benefit the working lives of library and archives workers. Along with Ray Pun, she is an editor of and author in *Career Transitions for Librarians: Proven Strategies for Finding Work in Another Type of Library*, published by Rowman & Littlefield in 2016. She is an SLA Rising Star and a 2012 *Library Journal* Mover & Shaker.

**Judy Anderson** is the Systemwide Access and Information Services librarian at Multnomah County Library. She has been a librarian for about 20 years. In her current role, she supports users with access issues, as well as supporting Bibliocommons and the Classic catalogue.

**Carson Block** has been a library technologist since the Web was a baby—as a library worker, IT director, and now a Library Technology consultant. His passions include leading technology visioning, planning, and other activities designed to help build the library's capacity to serve communities. He has been called "a geek who speaks English" and enjoys acting as a bridge between the worlds of librarians and hard-core technologists. He has a passion to de-mystify technology for the uninitiated, and to help IT professionals understand and support the goals of libraries. www.carsonblock.com/.

**Jill Castek** is the principal investigator for the Digital Equity in Libraries project and an associate professor of teaching, learning, and sociocultural studies at the University of Arizona. Her work examines the digital literacy acquisition process and digital problem solving among underrepresented adult learners.

**Shauna Edson** is one of two Digital Inclusion Fellows at the Salt Lake City Public Library. Her interest in digital inclusion stems from over four years of teaching, facilitating writing workshops and groups, coordinating volunteers, connecting with community partners, and working in traditional and digital literacies with the diverse communities that make up the Wasatch Front. She addresses concerns such as education without appropriation, accessibility, managing difficult conversations, and communication. Shauna is currently working toward an MS in communication with an emphasis on rhetoric and composition at the University of Utah. When Shauna is not on the trail, snow, or water, she lives in downtown Salt Lake City with her two boys and dog.

**Amanda Feist** is a librarian for the Workforce and Innovation Center at George Latimer Central Library. She has worked in urban libraries around the Twin Cities since 2009 and manages the Innovation Lab, a makerspace for adults.

**Cindy Fisher** is a library technology consultant for the Texas State Library and Archives Commission where she travels around the state to serve the needs of small and rural libraries with the You Can Do I.T. program. As a former learning technologies librarian, Cindy loves teaching technology and believes that empathy is the heart of teaching, along with equal doses of patience and curiosity.

**Erica Freudenberger** is a prolific collaborator who works with libraries to create community-led change. Currently the Outreach & Engagement consultant at the Southern Adirondack Library System, she formerly led the Red Hook Public Library, a finalist for *Library Journal*'s "Best Small Library Award," garnering five-star library ratings from 2013 to 2016. She took part in the *Re-envisioning Public Libraries* pilot with the Aspen Institute and the American Library Association's Libraries Transforming Communities initiative. She is a 2016 *Library Journal* Mover & Shaker.

**Cindy Gibbon** is Access and Information Services director for Multnomah County Library in Portland, Oregon. Throughout her long career she has promoted the role of the public library as a transformative force in the community. Her recent projects include opening the makerspace at the Rockwood Library and co-leading development and implementation of the Portland/ Multnomah County Digital Equity Action Plan. She holds a bachelor's degree from Pacific Lutheran University and a master's from the University of Pittsburgh Graduate School of Library and Information Science.

**Tommy Hamby** has been at the Salt Lake City Public Library for over 12 years, and he is currently the Adult Services coordinator at the Library. He oversees services and programs for adults in the Salt Lake City community. Some highlights of the innovative civic, practical, and fun programs Tommy has brought to the library include Rooftop Yoga, the Adult Spelling Bee, Utah's Trailblazing Women, Bike the Branches, and the Tech League. Tommy is passionate about serving his community and is currently working toward a Master of Public Administration at the University of Utah.

**Xenia Hernández** is an associate librarian in the Workforce and Innovation Center and helped open the Createch Studio and Arlington Hills Community Center in 2014.

**Amy Honisett** is the Public Training librarian at Multnomah County Library in Portland, Oregon, where she focuses on developing tools and training to help patrons learn about technology and gain job skills. She earned a Master of Art in English from Portland State University in Portland, Oregon, and a Master of Science in Library Science from Drexel University in Philadelphia, Pennsylvania.

**Gloria E. Jacobs** holds a Ph.D. in Teaching and Curriculum. Jacobs investigates adolescent, young adult, and adult use of digital technology and the implications of that use on individuals' lives. She has published articles in numerous professional journals and chapters in edited books. Jacobs splits her time as a researcher between Portland State University and the University of Arizona.

**Matthew Kopel** is a library and technology consultant based in Ithaca, NY. He serves as webmaster and technologist for the National Digital Inclusion Alliance. In 2017 he oversaw the Digital Inclusion Corps, a cooperative initiative between IMLS and NDIA.

**Alex Lent** is director of the Millis Public Library, president-elect of the Massachusetts Library Association, and founder/coordinator of the Library Directors Group. A frequent conference speaker, Lent has spoken at ALA-Midwinter, Computers in Libraries, the Small Libraries Forum, the New England Library Association Annual Conference, and many others in the United States and Canada.

**Maria Mucino** is the East Library Region manager at Maricopa County Library District. She manages four locations: Fountain Hills, Guadalupe, Queen Creek, and Robson Branch Libraries. Previous to that position, Maria was the branch manager at Guadalupe, a lead librarian at Mesa Public Library, a librarian at the United Nations Dag Hammarskjöld Library, a Library Coordinator at UNAM, and a research assistant at El Colegio de Mexico.

Maria believes that education disrupts poverty and within that access to new technologies is vital. She thrives on change and fiercely believes that libraries must deliver services based on community needs. Maria's passion to provide access to new technologies and STEM programming for underserved populations is second to none.

Maria received her master's degree in library science from the National Autonomous University of Mexico and The School of Information at Pratt Institute in New York City. She was part of the 1992–1993 Japan Foundation Cohort to attend the Japanese Language for Professional Librarians in Kita

Urawa, Japan. Maria has been awarded twice the Outreach Librarian of the Year, in 2003 and 2013 by the Arizona Library Association and earned three NACO Awards for Innovation in Library Programming.

**Lyndsey Runyan** is tasked with looking at how Multnomah County Library can reinvent library spaces for making, tinkering, and building community around DIY and technology skills. With an MLIS from the University of Washington and a background in Teen Services, Lyndsey's goal is to help design and implement sustainable, equitable, and engaging library spaces and services where the public can have fun diving into hands-on programming by investigating their own interests facilitated by library staff and volunteer mentors.

**Rebecca Ryan** has spent 13 years working inside and outside public libraries on issues of literacy, digital inclusion, and engagement. Previously the project manager for the mobile workplace, Ryan oversees the Rondo Library, bookmobile, community services, and workplace programming for the Saint Paul Public Library.

**Emily Scherer** is a relationship architect and local government leader for the Sierra Vista Public Library and Teen Center located in breathtaking Sierra Vista, Arizona. She manages the 30,000-plus-square-foot library in addition to designing innovative programs, creating opportunities for the library and wider community, and engaging staff and community to evolve the library as a community space for all.

Emily has written articles on librarianship, early literacy, engaging the public, and intentional networking, and has been published as a freelance writer in several local newspapers and magazines in addition to trade publications. Emily has spoken at various state and national conferences on topics ranging from library outreach to digital programs for the underserved. Emily is currently finishing her MPPA from Northwestern University, with a focus on how technology can benefit public policy.

**Elaine Stehel** studied French and Linguistics at the University of Utah, earning two Bachelor of Arts degrees and a TESOL certificate. Following over nine years teaching Beginning French and English as a Second Language to learners of all ages and abilities, Elaine joined the Salt Lake City Public Library's Main branch in the Circulation department in January 2016 and moved to the Nonfiction/Audiovisual department in October. When NTEN offered a second Digital Inclusion Fellowship at the Salt Lake City Public Library to begin in January 2017, Elaine applied and was asked to join The

City Library's Digital Inclusion efforts. Bringing her passion for teaching as well as community organizing and volunteer management to promote The City Library's Tech League, Elaine teaches and facilitates classes and Learning Circles and coordinates the Tech League volunteer program.

**Henry Stokes** is a library technology consultant at the Texas State Library and Archives Commission. He provides training and consulting for library staff across the state with a focus on emerging technology trends and broadband connectivity. As State E-rate coordinator for Texas, he supports public libraries participating in the E-rate telecommunications discount program.

**Marika Stoloch**'s passion for social justice led her to libraries where she started the first homework center at the Saint Paul Public Library in 2001. Since then she worked as a girls' engineering camp director; a library associate; an English teacher; and is now the Youth Services Coordinator at the Saint Paul Public Library. As youth services manager she helped develop the award-winning one-book program Read Brave, established the teen tinkering space Createch, and launched Library Go which connects all Saint Paul Public School students with a virtual library card. She lives in Saint Paul and keeps curiosity alive through adventures with her wife and two kids.

**Matthew Timberlake** is the Information Technology portfolio manager for Multnomah County Library. He is a founding member of the Digital Inclusion Network in Portland. His work as a technologist has been featured in national publications in both the United States and the United Kingdom.

**Steve Teeri** has created two library makerspaces from the ground up, at both the Detroit Public Library and the Ann Arbor District Library. Steve has also worked with organizations including ALA, PLA, the U.S. State Department, the University of Michigan School of Information, and the Harvard Graduate School of Education. His greatest joy is teaching people new skills, and learning more himself along the way. His son, Kellen, can now beat him in a foot race.

**Pang Yang** is the Community Services coordinator for the Saint Paul Public Library. She manages the Mobile Workplace and citywide programming in multiple languages. Yang is an avid mug collector and likes to travel.

**Ricci Yuhico** originally wanted to be a teacher but found that being a librarian was pretty much a dream job come true. She has had the privilege of making and facilitating teen spaces, from YOUmedia Miami in the Miami-Dade Public Library System to The Studio in Broward County Library. She believes in the necessity and power of having teen spaces equipped with resources and dedicated teen-focused staff in libraries, most especially in large urban systems. While tinkering with tech is certainly exciting, the capacity to be a positive and empowering mentor in the lives of youth is by far the greatest gift she's received in working in this field.

She is currently the managing librarian for Young Adult Services at the Mid-Manhattan Library of The New York Public Library, but avidly reps her hometown of Miami.